FEB   2018

THE
STOWAWAY

A YOUNG MAN'S EXTRAORDINARY
ADVENTURE TO ANTARCTICA

LAURIE GWEN SHAPIRO

SIMON & SCHUSTER

NEW YORK   LONDON   TORONTO   SYDNEY   NEW DELHI

Simon & Schuster
1230 Avenue of the Americas
New York, NY 10020

First Simon & Schuster hardcover edition January 2018

SIMON & SCHUSTER and colophon are registered trademarks of Simon & Schuster, Inc.

For information about special discounts for bulk purchases, please contact Simon & Schuster Special Sales at 1-866-506-1949 or business@simonandschuster.com.

The Simon & Schuster Speakers Bureau can bring authors to your live event. For more information or to book an event, contact the Simon & Schuster Speakers Bureau at 1-866-248-3049 or visit our website at www.simonspeakers.com.

Interior design by Ruth Lee-Mui

Manufactured in the United States of America

1   3   5   7   9   10   8   6   4   2

Library of Congress Cataloging-in-Publication Data

Names: Shapiro, Laurie Gwen, author.
Title: The stowaway : a young man's extraordinary adventure to Antarctica / Laurie Gwen Shapiro.
Description: First Simon & Schuster hardcover edition. | New York : Simon & Schuster, 2018. | "Simon & Schuster nonfiction original hardcover"—Title page verso. | Includes bibliographical references and index.
Identifiers: LCCN 2017007428 (print) | LCCN 2017010926 (ebook) | ISBN 9781476753867 (hardcover : alkaline paper) | ISBN 9781476753881 (Ebook)
Subjects: LCSH: Antarctica—Description and travel. | Gawronski, Billy, 1910–1981—Travel—Antarctica. | Stowaways—Antarctica—Biography. | Ocean travel—History—20th century. | Adventure and adventurers—Antarctica—Biography. | Teenage boys—New York (State)—New York—Biography.
Classification: LCC G875.G38 S53 2018 (print) | LCC G875.G38 (ebook) | DDC 919.8904—dc23
LC record available at https://lccn.loc.gov/2017007428

ISBN 978-1-4767-5386-7
ISBN 978-1-4767-5388-1 (ebook)

Dedicated to my father

JULIUS SHAPIRO

my hero and lifelong champion.

All that is personal soon rots;
it must be packed in ice or salt.

—William Butler Yeats

CONTENTS

THE
STOWAWAY

PROLOGUE

With his back against the sunset, a seventeen-year-old boy lingered on the docks along the Hudson River. By his calculations, it was a ten-minute swim from where he stood to the ship.

The new high school graduate waited, his soft grey eyes fixed on the *City of New York*, moored and heavily guarded on the Hoboken piers. The sun went down at six forty-five this day—August 24, 1928—but still he fought back his adrenaline. He wanted true darkness before carrying out his plan. At noon the next day, the ship would leave New York Harbor and sail nine thousand miles to the frozen continent of Antarctica, the last frontier on Earth left to explore. He intended to be aboard.

That summer, baby-faced Billy Gawronski was three inches short of his eventual height of five foot eleven, and his voice still squeaked.

"You are a late bloomer," his doting immigrant mother told him in thickly accented English. Yet the ambitious dreamer, born and raised in the gritty tenement streets of the Lower East Side, was as familiar with Commander Richard Evelyn Byrd's flagship as any reporter assigned to cover its launch. The Antarctica-bound barquentine was an old-fashioned multi-masted ship that suggested the previous century, with enchanting square sails arranged against an almost impenetrable maze of ropes. The 161-foot wooden vessel spanned half a city block, her 27-foot beam taller than a three-story building. Sail- and steam-powered and weighing 200 tons, with sturdy wooden sides 34 inches thick, she had seen duty as an Arctic icebreaker for Norwegian seal hunters starting in 1885. On one run in icy waters in 1912, her captain had been the last to see the *Titanic*; just ten miles away, he'd been afraid to help the sinking ship, as he was hunting illegally in territorial waters. Like so many immigrants, the ship once known as *Samson* found her name changed when she arrived in America in 1928, becoming the *City of New York*. She was the most romantic of the four boats in Byrd's cobbled-together flotilla, and the one leaving first—with the greatest fanfare—early the next afternoon.

Several times in his mind that evening, Billy dove into the Hudson and started swimming, only to find his feet firmly on land. But he had been on board the SS *New York* before. Nine days earlier, he and two thousand other New Yorkers had taken the Fourteenth Street Ferry to Hoboken, New Jersey, and gaped at the *City of New York*, moored next to the grand Dutch ocean liner the SS *Veendam*. The crowd was wowed with anticipation. Just past noon, the ship's captain, Frederick Melville—second cousin of the nineteenth-century author Herman Melville—gave the okay, waving the first sweaty guests up the gangway, their dollar admission supporting the Byrd Antarctica expedition's fund-raising drive. Several members of Melville's crew, including the chief engineer, Thomas "Mac" Mulroy, and sixty-year-old veteran sailmaker John Jacobson, joined him in greeting the adoring public. No, he told them, Byrd was not aboard. Everyone still wanted to gawk.

When it had been Billy's turn to board, he'd wandered the wooden decks, still cargo free to accommodate guests. The poop aft (rear deck) was elevated, housing Commander Byrd's cabin, an elegant wood-paneled chart room, and a state-of-the-art radio room with technology that would let the explorers be heard no matter how far they sailed. Under the poop deck were spaces for the machine room and the radio generator. One level down were seven cabins—the cramped quarters where the men would sleep—as well as several storerooms, and lockers for holding mops and paint. He stood in the machine room with other tourists—men and women content to admire all the nifty gadgets. Also aft were the ship's engine and oppressively hot boiler room.

None of these places had been right for a hiding spot. Forward proved more promising, with its large fo'c'sle (forecastle, a front deck), and a second, smaller fo'c'sle in the peak: a narrow hollow under the bowsprit (a thick pole projecting from the upper end of a sailing vessel) of the boat's prow (the part of the bow above the water). Here, under this second hidden fo'c'sle, Billy had spied a good-sized space in a shelf. The exposed top fo'c'sle would be visible to anyone on the ship during the departure ceremonies, but the second fo'c'sle would remain dark. Satisfied with his investigation, the lad grabbed one of the commemorative paper cups set aside as a souvenir before heading for the ramp.

Afterward, still on a high, Billy had walked the New Jersey shoreline until he'd scouted the lookout site he was in now, a long distance from the ship but not out of reach for a superior swimmer like himself. Another ocean liner had taken the *Veendam*'s place next to the expedition ship in Hoboken's busy Pier 1: the SS *Leviathan*, headed overseas the next day, too. The *Leviathan* dwarfed its famous ice-bound companion vessel in dock.

With the twilight not yet dissipated, Billy still had an excellent view of the many ships going up and down the brackish southern-flowing Hudson. Could a ship hit him as he swam? He ate what little food he'd brought: an apple and an egg salad sandwich. As for what he would eat after that? He hadn't bothered to think about it.

Even under the dimming sky, Billy could make out the shadowed bodies of stationed watchmen, but he was unsure if they were Byrd's crew or borrowed Coast Guards keeping vigil. There would be no sneaking up the gangway, the narrow metal plank for boarding. He would have to swim out to the unprotected side of the ship, the side facing the water. Who would think to guard the edges of the ship away from the pier? Once aboard, he did not have a sure grasp on how he would reveal himself to Commander Byrd or justify his presence on the expedition, but he trusted he could wing it.

In Byrd, Americans like Billy now had a superexplorer of their own—someone who could stand proudly beside England's legendary Ernest Shackleton and Robert Falcon Scott, not to mention Norway's Roald Amundsen, the crafty strategist who in 1911 had been the first to reach the South Pole, just five weeks ahead of Scott's team. The thirty-nine-year-old blueblood Virginian "Dick" Byrd was a slight but strong man with a chiseled, smooth-shaven face. He looked the part of a hero and acted like one, too, admired already for the responsible, safety-first ethics he had demonstrated exploring the North Pole by ship and plane in 1926. Now he had set his eye on the South.

Byrd's team would be the first American expedition to Antarctica since Lieutenant Charles Wilkes and his exploring party poked around the coast eighty-eight years before, in February 1840. And Wilkes had not even set foot on the continent itself.

When the commander's four ships reached Antarctica, the coldest, windiest outpost imaginable, he would unload a specially designed Ford trimotor three-propeller transport plane with a seventy-foot wingspan—the first commercial aircraft sturdy enough to weather a 120-mile-per-hour flight over the South Pole; only 199 of the planes were manufactured. The wings and fuselage were constructed from corrugated duralumin, a light, strong alloy of aluminum, copper, manganese, and magnesium, while the landing gear and bracing were all steel. Byrd's underlings would assemble it on the ice barrier that guarded the continent of Antarctica, and, with the aid of a pilot, he would fly over the polar plateau, proudly dropping the Stars and Stripes from the sky. Two more monoplanes (a plane with only one set of wings) were sailing on other ships farther southbound to 90 degrees south: a small Fokker and an even smaller Fairchild. With the introduction of airplanes to Antarctica, Byrd and his pilots would have the first bird's-eye views of its great mysterious interior, and no doubt add to the fragmentary maps of the south polar region, a landmass Byrd believed to be greater than that of the United States and Mexico combined—at least five million miles. But as Billy told his family and friends, no one was sure.

Breathless articles in prominent publications such as *Scientific American* and *Popular Mechanics* heralded the dawn of the mechanical age of exploration and asked readers with the sketchiest knowledge of Antarctica to imagine a pilot seeing the United States from the air for the first time, spotting a Grand Canyon here, a buffalo herd there. Was Antarctica home to animals that had never been seen? Indigenous people? Lost dinosaurs?

Even Billy's Polish grandmother, with her rudimentary English, agreed that it was marvelous to be living in an age when man could do such things as fly over a frozen continent. So why did everyone except his *babcia* scoff whenever Billy said he wanted to have a life as adventurous as Byrd's?

In the rags-to-riches decade of the 1920s, everyone in the papers seemed to be living big, meaningful lives, from slugger Babe Ruth, to fashionable Coco Chanel, to comic genius Charlie Chaplin. Jews and blacks had broken through: the Marx Brothers achieved overnight fame after their Broadway debut, and provocative entertainer Josephine Baker packed them in at Paris's Folies Bergère. New York City in 1928 was the rolling-in-the-dough town immortalized by F. Scott Fitzgerald, whose smash 1920 debut novel, *This Side of Paradise*, was assigned to English classes at Billy's alma mater, Manhattan's progressive Textile High School. Adults, or at least city dwellers, were having a grand old time; only the most sober investors knew that the stock market was not on a permanent high.

Even once-penniless immigrants were doing better for themselves. Billy knew he would inherit the one-man interior decorating business his father had established after arriving in New York as a destitute young man. Now that his boy would graduate in four short years from Cooper Union, a prestigious, free college in Greenwich Village, Rudy Gawronski was ready to add "and Son" to his sign. Billy's application to Cooper Union had been decent; he supposed he had a knack for art as well as history and languages, but who wanted to study history when you could make history? The thought of a humdrum future stuffing furniture mortified him.

By nearly nine o'clock on that August night, darkness draped the sky, and lights began to sparkle on in the new downtown skyscrapers— young, electric edifices from a decade of big money. From where he crouched, Billy could see the pyramid atop the Bankers Trust Company Building on Wall Street; the wedding-cake-shaped thirty-story Standard Oil Building on lower Broadway; the forty-story Ritz Tower on Park Avenue; and the first of the city's Art Deco towers, such as the New York Telephone Building on West Street, completed just months before. Great buildings that proved great things were possible.

Billy stayed awake hours into the night, guessing and second-guessing the right moment to jump off the pier. Glory was not for the skittish, he told himself. Still, he was scared about low visibility under blackened skies; afraid that he might lose his way and drown, although he'd easily managed dozens of river swims with his athletic father and with his downtown friends. But was anyone more determined than Billy to hitch a ride on the most famous rig in America? It was the bold, he was certain, who won the right to adventure.

A few minutes past four in the morning, he'd had enough waiting. The young man took a breath and plunged.

ONE

THE GOLDEN DOOR

In 1907 dark-haired, mustached Rudolf Gawronski left Stanisławowo for New York at the age of nineteen. Billy's future father traveled alone on the SS *Campania*, setting out from a Poland partitioned by the Hapsburg rulers of Austria to seek his fortune. The adventuresome textiles apprentice cleared Ellis Island in an old-fashioned suit and gladly took to a relative's couch in a third-floor walk-up on East Eighteenth Street, near Gramercy Park. His cousin suggested he borrow some newfangled clothes and that Americans would like him better if he called himself Rudy.

He had not turned his back on all he'd left behind. Back in Europe, he'd courted pretty fifteen-year-old Fromia Zajac, baby sister of a friend, visiting her in Czernowice—a city under Austro-Hungarian rule—and leaving her with a memorable kiss. Rudy had not forgotten that she'd expressed interest in leaving for America, too. From his new city of residence, he maintained a flirtatious international postcard exchange with the girl. Fromia was not Rudy's first love. He had also left behind a daughter named Stefanie under his parents' care. When he became a widower is not known, nor is even the name of his first wife, but the mother of Stefanie was certainly not the young Fromia, who sent "real photo" postcards to Rudy's first permanent New York address: c/o Deutsch Brothers, 319 Houston Street, on the Lower East Side. These hand-tinted postcards made from photographs of the sender showed Fromia to be movie-star slim with an ample bosom, her lips parted suggestively.

Deutsch Brothers was both a private banking concern and an interior decorating business. Rudy lived for more than a year in this basement superintendent's apartment, until he was promoted from janitor to shop assistant and had enough for a better place. (He had worked as an interior decoration apprentice back in the old country.)

Not so long later, on April 6, 1909, the proudly literate Rudy would have read local Polish-language articles celebrating Admiral Robert Peary, an American navy man who claimed to be first to visit the geographical North Pole: a wet landscape dotted with floating ice. He had made the journey on foot, aided by a forty-three-year-old black man named Matthew Henson and four Inuit assistants. After Peary's return, the US Congress promoted him to rear admiral, and New York's members-only Explorers Club named him president. But a New York surgeon named Frederick Cook publicly challenged Peary's claim, insisting that *he* was the man who had been there first—in 1908—along with two Inuit. Cook's assertion infuriated Admiral Peary. Their supporters would dispute their achievements for months to come, a battle that researchers continued into later years. Most historians now believe *neither* explorer made it—both guilty of fudging coordinates for glory.

Rudy soon had more personal news: Fromia had said yes! He was getting a bride. In the fall of 1909, Fromia Zajac was vetted for disease and mental health, and on the same day, released from Ellis Island. Her "Rudy" waited for his seventeen-year-old fiancée past the immigration guards, where Fromia fell into her lover's arms. Rudy couldn't believe his luck. The chesty girl of five foot eight was more beautiful than he remembered. He encouraged her to quickly Anglicize her name, suggesting she go with Francesca, which, she agreed, sounded elegant. Scandal would dog them if she moved into his place before their wedding, so he had found her a temporary apartment at 57 First Avenue, in the Polish swath of Manhattan's Lower East Side. He'd paid the first month's rent.

An alderman at city hall wed the couple on December 30, 1909, and Francesca relocated to Rudy's unimpressive one-room place at 165 Avenue A, with a bathtub in the hallway and a tiny kitchenette. On the bright side, the apartment was closer to the then-powerful St. Stanislaus Parish on East Seventh Street, the center of the Manhattan Polish community.

Imagine the sexual frustrations of a Catholic churchgoing couple of the era. Finally, on the last nights of 1909, they lay together. A son was born on September 10, 1910, nine months after their wedding night. Rudy let his wife pick the name to honor members of her family: William Gregory. They called him Billy—a good American name. The happy threesome took weekend trips to family-friendly sights accessible by trolley car or subway: Coney Island, and the Central Park and Bronx Zoos. Stefanie, Billy's half sister left behind in Poland, would not arrive on American shores until 1929. For twenty years, Billy would be raised as a cosseted only child.

Francesca gained significant weight in pregnancy and continued to put on the pounds during the first few years of child rearing. Meanwhile, Rudy, a rugged five foot eleven, was exercising and in the best shape of his life. The once-happy couple began to bicker over domestic issues, especially with an exploratory toddler in the mix. Partly to escape quarrels at home, Rudy joined men's groups, and Francesca volunteered as much as she could, especially for the Red Cross.

In Billy's early childhood, Rudy found steady work as an interior designer and restorer of fine antique furniture in other people's firms. He also secured a few independent clients, which let him put away extra for a rainy day. The Gawronskis soon had enough money saved so that Francesca could travel home to show off her child to her extended family back in Europe.

Rudy, grateful for a respite from fighting, decided to stay put in New York—ostensibly to head off cash-flow problems. Only mother and son traveled across the Atlantic Ocean via the steamship SS *Patricia*, a passenger line built for the Hamburg American Steamship Company. While there are postcards between husband and wife during this yearlong separation, the once-spicy content from their days of transatlantic courtship is conspicuously missing.

This early oceanic trip thrilled Billy, though, and after his months at sea as a three- and then four-year-old, he refused to take off his sailing suit. When anyone asked the articulate little boy, who could already read and write, what he wanted to be when he grew up, his mother answered for him: "He wants to be a sailor."

Billy smiled big in several photos taken upon his return to New York: on top of a pony in the East Village; astride other of the city's horses. Police officers were happy to indulge his cheeky requests, happy to show off their horses, delighting in a little boy so fearless.

The Gawronskis settled back into their lives near the Polish National Home, or as they called it, the Polski Dom Narodowy. This community center at the heart of a ten-block Polish neighborhood of tenement buildings centered on St. Mark's Place on the Lower East Side, where neighborhood stores catered to homesick Polish-speaking residents, with *pączki* (jelly doughnuts) in bakery windows. Friends of friends held Bible study, and singing society get-togethers, and meetings of the men's club to which Rudy now devoted most of his time: a gymnastic and political society called Dom Narodowy Sokot, or the Polish Falcons of America.

An American outgrowth of a paramilitary fraternal organization started in Poland in 1867, the Polish Falcons adopted a strenuous program of physical education to do their part in bringing on "Polish national rejuvenation through self-discipline and physical fitness." The falcon was chosen as a symbol of strength and self-preservation. Fittingly for a society named after a bird, each group was called a nest. The first was founded in 1887, in Chicago, and soon there were twelve nests across the United States; the one on the Lower East Side was called Falcons Nest 7. In Polish-language handouts, the Falcons stated that they hoped to "exert every possible influence towards attaining political independence of the fatherland," then under the governance of the Austro-Hungarian Empire. They fought for their adoptive homeland, too. Throughout the twentieth century, many brawny Falcons ranked as officers, in peacetime and in both world wars, where they proved among the fiercest Americans in battle.

Rudy, doing his small part to rebuild the Polish spirit, went to the gym religiously and took daily swims at the closest public pool. He never missed rowdy outings to Brooklyn's Coney Island, at the edge of the Atlantic Ocean—and the group swims that took place even in the middle of the winter, with plenty of vodka to help the shock of the cold. Billy was excited to tag along on these manly swims. When the well-liked Rudy was voted in as president of Nest 7, he made sure his child learned not only to speak Polish fluently but also—and in some ways, more importantly to him—to swim better than anyone else. Billy was an impressive swimmer by the age of six.

To give her son an outlet for his considerable boy energy, Francesca enrolled him in free acting classes offered by the church community. Amusing photos of the "actor" were pasted into a family album: Billy dressed in Polish national costume, as a soldier, and even as an Indian.

A handful of especially precocious children were asked to recite poetry in front of the great pianist, composer, and political activist Ignacy Jan Paderewski, who was visiting the St. Stanislaus Parish to garner American support for an independent Poland. Billy was a natural selection. For years to come, his father clung to this favorite story about his son, telling new decorating clients how the great composer Paderewski complimented him on his boy's recitation. As a grown man, Billy would recall, "The parish was the heart of my parents' world and kept us going as a family."

Polish politics were always on the lips of his parents' friends. Fortunately, the kid with a notorious appetite had plenty to eat while waiting for never-ending partisan arguments to stop. Ladies in his church loved the way he complimented them at get-togethers, and they competed for his attention, waving and calling him over to try their home-cooked dishes. Potlucks were the highlights of church fetes, and each week, Billy stuffed his plate with competing offerings: a hunter's stew called *bigos*; stuffed cabbage with mushroom sauce; a potato-lamb soup called *żurek* (served up in a scooped-out loaf of rye bread); white borscht soured by sauerkraut; and comforting pierogies stuffed with each woman's special filling, savory (meat, potato, kasha, sauerkraut with mushrooms or spinach) or sweet (cherry, blueberry, or white curd cheese). There were heaping servings of beef goulash and pork schnitzel topped with egg, and *ogórki kiszone* (dill pickles). But Billy always kept room in his belly for kielbasa, the spicy Polish sausage, which would be his favorite treat for a lifetime.

Although the Gawronskis were among the most active parishioners of the church, they decided their child was better off in local Public School 64 on East Sixth Street. They wanted Billy to gain a native speaker's advantage in their adopted country. But they signed him up for Sunday Polish classes, which turned out to be enough; he soon amused extended family members by telling long jokes in fluent Polish. Over his lifetime, he would master five languages.

In 1918 the Gawronskis moved to yet another railroad flat, at 233 East Ninth Street, careful to rent in their parish. Even with two tiny bedrooms instead of one big one, life with an eight-year-old boy was still cramped.

By 1920, Rudy was yearning for open space and wanting desperately to move back to the reborn Second Polish Republic, which had come into being in November 1918, in the wake of World War I. Rudy's hero, General Józef Piłsudski, had recruited the great Paderewski to become the new prime minister. Although the virtuoso wasn't used to handling political crises, he would keep the position for almost a year before resuming his musical career, for which he had a well-deserved fanatical following.

Francesca preferred to stay put in a free America with its mind-boggling radio technology—a nation teeming with shops that sold things she actually wanted. Why go backward? To keep his struggling marriage, Rudy yielded first but decided he at least needed to see a free Poland once with his own eyes. In May 1922 he left New York with his émigré brother Walter aboard the *Frederik VIII* for a half-year visit back home. When he returned, there was still fighting, and financial struggle, and he and Francesca put off having more children.

But an active boy such as Billy needed company. Over the next few years, the parents agreed to a cat, a snake, rats, and, finally, a dog. Enter Tootsie, a stray black-and-white mutt. Animal rights crusading had recently taken hold in New York, and a new sort of dog show had been organized by the New York Women's League for Animals. Unlike the Westminster Kennel Club Dog Show at Madison Square Garden (then on Twenty-Sixth Street and Madison Avenue), which catered to fancy breeds, this one, held way downtown in a working-class neighborhood near Lafayette Street, gave prizes to stray animals that had been adopted into loving homes. Fourteen-year-old Billy was keen to have his Tootsie compete in the contest, confident he was a sure bet to win. What other dog had been trained to ride a horse? He had worked all year with a milkman he'd befriended; horses helped deliver milk bottles, clopping along the streets among the city's growing number of motorcars. The man had laughed when Billy asked if he could put his dog on his horse. Tootsie's triumph on April 21, 1925, was covered in the *New York Daily News* and the *New York Daily Sun*. Billy, as he'd promised to his peers, had demolished the competition. He ate up the attention at school and also at home, where his mother proudly clipped her son's delightful achievement for her still-thin scrapbook. In a few years, it would become a lot thicker.

At fifteen, Billy had an exciting new hobby: girls. Pocket money was desperately needed so he could ask female classmates to soda shops and silent movies without begging his father for a buck. His way with languages helped his search for an after-school job. Not many Catholics had a solid grasp of Yiddish from the street, but he did, thanks to his many Lower East Side stickball friends. Besides, Yiddish was so close to German, which he'd mastered in school. Jewish parents shook their heads in disbelief at a Catholic Pole's lovely Yiddish, and had a proposal for him. Did he want to earn a dollar? Billy was soon in high demand as a *Shabbos* goy: a non-Jew hired for a bit of spare money to put lights on in Jewish homes on Friday nights and Saturdays, when the observant are forbidden by Jewish law to use electricity on the Sabbath.

Meanwhile, Rudy was growing more frustrated with his overcrowded living situation. What kind of success story was he if he still lived in a Lower East Side tenement? He had long dreamed of his own mom-and-pop interior decoration business, and was grooming Billy to be his partner and heir. He wanted his son to go to college, learn the new business ways; then his Billy would join him, and they would build a mini-empire together. When the pickiest customers of his firm needed a master upholsterer for everything from drapes, to ottomans, to velvet chesterfield sofas, they always asked for the "Polish man." Boasting to Francesca that he had enough clients and money in the bank, Rudy insisted he was ready to give it a go as a solo contractor. Many of his forward-thinking clients had started out poor; they would support a man who thought big. And it was a good time for an ambitious businessman. Investors were buying stocks with gusto. People buy a lot of furniture when they're making a lot of money, and, by 1926, there was a citywide economic flush. Fruit mongers from Little Italy now owned large groves in Florida after speculating on land. Jews owned stores they'd once worked at. America loved strivers.

When Rudy investigated storefront options outside the neighborhood, he didn't mention his field trips, with good reason: his wife had happily found her own set of friends in Manhattan, mostly through the Red Cross, where she held an officer position. Francesca had been a budding suffragette and was quick to join the Democratic Party shortly after women won the right to vote in 1920 with the passage of the Nineteenth Amendment. She had joined the local ladies' political club, too. Rudy feared her reaction to his desire to move the family away.

He was also finding his teenage son increasingly defiant, and on several occasions threatened a lashing when the boy played hooky from school. Because of Billy's sophomore year finals, Rudy wouldn't let him go to Richard Byrd's parade on June 23, 1926, after having returned from the North Pole. What was more important, a parade or grades? Even in an era of triumphant tickertape parades for the likes of superstar athletes—including one that July for American golfer Bobby Jones, winner of the prestigious British Open; and one several months earlier for sea captain George Fried, who, with his heroic crew of the American luxury liner SS *President Roosevelt*, had rescued the sinking British steam cargo ship *Antinoe* in a winter hurricane—Byrd's had been a noteworthy one to miss. The aviator had claimed a spectacular first aerial dash over the pole with his flying pal Floyd Bennett—although gadflies were already hinting that Byrd fudged the coordinates to heighten his profile. Nevertheless, most of America took Byrd's word for it.

Rudy's widowed mother was also newly arrived from Poland, bringing with her a collection of amulets and a rich set of old-world traditions, such as telling the family's fortunes from dripped candle wax and tea leaves. Rudy quickly had it up to here with the old woman stuck in her superstitious ways. Between her, his rebellious teenager, and the newly politicized wife, there was nowhere to go but the living room. Rudy, a traditionalist, believed in staying with a woman; especially the mother of his son. But he was more convinced than ever that he should find them a place to live with more space. Why not just get his mother her own floor? That might quell Francesca's concerns about her mother-in-law's interference.

Still, it moved Rudy how tender his dear mother was with her only grandson. Billy always called Rudy's mother Babcia, never Grandma, and she was so proud that her American grandson spoke to her in perfect Polish. When Babcia pinched her grandson's prominent apple cheeks, kissing him on the head, Billy was anything but embarrassed. The stubborn modern youth and his antique grandmother with yellowed teeth and a crystal ball were the unlikeliest of allies.

Without Francesca, Rudy continued to take secret subway rides to Bayside, in Queens, after hearing of a thriving, small Polish community centered around the St. Josaphat Parish. The boxlike one-story church was erected in 1901 to serve the determined Polish who had left the crowded Lower East Side for the outer borough. There was also a pleasingly active Bayside Polish Democratic Club. Rudy braced himself for a fight at home and told his wife that he had already befriended the club president, John Stroebel, who knew every Pole in town—a connection he was sure would bring bread-and-butter upholstery customers to his door until the neighborhood's movie stars called on him for interior decoration.

In the end, he was the husband, the breadwinner, and he had final say.

Rudy avoided buying in Bayside's "Polack Town"—where the Negro families lived, too—fearing it might turn off snobby clients. He picked a roomy house located in the business district: a green-and-white single-family dwelling with a half-story attic and a storefront on the bottom floor for his business. The address, 4021 First Street at Ahles Road, was almost the farthest you could get from Manhattan without leaving Queens, but it was still within New York City, so Billy could continue to attend his excellent all-borough public high school. It would now be an hour ride into Manhattan, but it was easily accessible by the Long Island Railroad. He didn't have to lose any friends.

To quell Francesca's worries about losing her own friends, Rudy maintained that it would be a close enough walk to the new Polish church and club meetings. And so many people she knew were moving here, too! Fifteen thousand people lived in Bayside, double the number of a year before. Their new home wasn't fancy like the grand estates near the Bayside Yacht Club, but it was convenient if she wanted to get into Manhattan without a car. It was only two blocks from the railroad, and it would be theirs alone—a triumph for two people who'd each arrived at Ellis Island with zilch.

As added incentive, Rudy promised animal-mad Billy that he could set up a tiny bee apiary on their property; understandably, he had refused to do so in a Manhattan apartment despite the books Billy had excitedly checked out of the library. Not only that, Rudy would help his son learn the craft that he knew from his youth in Poland. Billy couldn't believe it: an apiary!

The Gawronskis took out a mortgage and moved in weeks later. They soon bought a car: a brand-new Ford Model A.

Francesca made it known that her boy would have plenty of time to learn the interior decoration trade later. The new apprentice-type errands Rudy demanded cut into the time Billy could spend reading in the library like he had back in Manhattan. Billy agreed with his mother, thrilled that he'd found a branch library down the block from his new home. As was his gregarious way, he befriended the female librarian, who routinely put aside Jack London, Joseph Conrad, and Herman Melville for him. She soon learned that he liked any literature about adventure, really, especially to the polar regions, the least-explored lands on Earth. Adventure novels had been popular with boys since the early nineteenth century, and with the advent of long-distance flight, the mid-1920s was a particularly rich time for the genre. Such books led many an inner-city working-class boy like Billy to feel that he could achieve his dreams.

Billy's favorite librarian secured him an early copy of *Dick Byrd: Air Explorer*, an authorized biography in a series for boys that touted recent escapades by the most heroic. Roy Chapman Andrews discovered petrified eggs of a "million-year-old dinosaur"—he would later become director of the American Museum of Natural History; affluent Manhattanite (and great-great-grandson of Commodore Cornelius Vanderbilt) Douglas Burden encountered the nine-foot-long giant lizards of Komodo Island; Massachusetts Institute of Technology graduate R. Oglesby Marsh led a Central American expedition that brought back living specimens of "white" Indians of Panama's Darién Gap to the Smithsonian Institution in Washington, DC. All were thrilling reads, but the book about his personal hero—which was reprinted five times in quick succession—captivated Billy most of all.

Time in the library, fine. What kind of father would argue with that? But now that the boy was sixteen, Rudy expected Billy to increase his responsibilities, starting with accompanying him in the new automobile to deliver finished work to clients. Why break his back when he had a strong son to balance the load?

The upstart decorator had perfected the contemporary look of 1926. He wasn't stuck in the frilly Edwardian or Art Nouveau style some of his competitors were. With a few wealthy clients to his name, Rudy set his sights on an even richer celebrity clientele. There were still plenty to be found in Bayside: in response to rumors earlier in the decade of a third major New York City film studio being built in Brooklyn, the silent-film stars of the metropolis had joined in a mad rush to grab homes.

The first luminary to arrive and elevate Bayside's reputation had been boxer-turned-actor James J. Corbett, who purchased 221-04 Thirty-Sixth Avenue, a Queen Anne–style house, with his second wife, Vera, in 1902. Corbett was a household name far beyond the two-block Bayside stretch that would one day be renamed Corbett Road. Nicknamed Gentleman Jim for his gracious manner, he was originally a bank clerk and was whispered to have had a college education. Way back in 1892, Corbett had knocked out the great John

L. Sullivan in the twenty-first round to become the world heavy-weight champion.

Billy and his parents were surrounded by glamour just out of reach. Their lower-middle-class Bayside neighbors called the nearby posh stretch overlooking Crocheron Park "Actors Row"—understandable when this family of movie lovers took roll call of the colony of silent-film stars who lived there or had until recently. Comic actor and director Buster Keaton, nicknamed "the Great Stone Face" for his signature deadpan expression, was one of the bigger names. Gloria Swanson was as revered for her clothing choices as for her romantic leads. Bayside was also home to John Barrymore and his wife, the "Goddess of the Silver Screen," Dolores Costello, whom he'd met (and begun an affair with) filming 1926's *The Sea Beast*, a loose adaptation of Melville's *Moby-Dick*—Barrymore played Captain Ahab. Costello was the daughter of another prominent Bayside resident: the first matinee star, Maurice Costello, who back in 1911 had starred in an adaptation of Charles Dickens's French Revolution novel *A Tale of Two Cities*.

Bayside was secluded but a handy enough commute to Astoria, Queens, home of the Famous Players–Lasky Corporation (soon to be renamed Paramount Pictures) and the Kaufman studios, and also to Vitagraph Studios in South Greenfield, Brooklyn (a neighborhood now called Midwood), which was rapidly losing its woodsy setting for outdoor films to highways and automobiles. Not long before the Gawronskis arrived in Queens, Warner Bros. had bought Vitagraph and moved most of its operations to the more bucolic Hollywood, with the exception of a few Vitaphone short subjects shot until they closed shop altogether in 1939. Producer-director D. W. Griffith still filmed in New York City—even in Bayside—although his box-office pull was waning a decade after *The Birth of a Nation* and *Intolerance*. *The Jazz Singer*, the first all-talkie feature-length film, premiered in 1927 at the newly opened Tower Theatre in Los Angeles, the first cinema specifically designed for these revolutionary chatty films, to unqualified success. The industry was going in a new direction—and out of Brooklyn. The rumored new studio had not yet materialized (and never would), and the glitterati had started a steady exodus to California.

Francesca was spooked. Rudy, however, wasn't worried about Los Angeles's rise, reminding his wife that the economy was still booming. And even if all the actors left, more rich people would buy their homes and want new tables and chairs. They were in the upholstery business, not the film business.

And for the time being, anyway, there were still actors around. Classes didn't mix much in 1920s Bayside, but sixteen-year-old Billy saw the occasional star when he went to the local Capitol Theatre a few blocks from his home for vaudeville acts and motion pictures.

Some of the more developed boys his age were having more luck snagging dates to the movies; unfortunately for Billy, he desired girls more than they liked him. He was a great friend to have, and they might go out with him to be nice, but he was still so short and boyish, with a squeaky voice. Because he'd stayed enrolled in his Manhattan school, it was hard to meet local girls. On weekends especially, there was time to kill. When he wasn't at the local library, he often hung around the firemen at Bayside's Hook and Ladder 152 and Engine Company 306 on 214th Place and Griffin Avenue. Billy learned their terminology—words such as *pumper engine* and *pumper truck*—and one fireman let him hold a smoke mask in his hands. Pleased by his curiosity, the men encouraged him to consider a life as a firefighter when he was old enough. He said he would think about it; he did want adventure.

What every immigrant to New York craved was security, including Rudy Gawronski, who had no desire for a rootless existence. He was proud to have finally arrived in the (lower) middle class. Billy, however, let it be known that he preferred Manhattan to Queens, even with his friends at the library and the firehouse. One year, two years after he had left the Lower East Side, it was still where he felt most at home. Bayside was so far out in Queens that most kids didn't know he was still in New York City; his old grade-school friends teased him about wherever the hell he was living these days.

Textile High on Manhattan's West Eighteenth Street was a competitive trade school where Billy specialized in interior decoration to please his father. He had a solid B average, with his highest marks in history and languages, but also more than one C. His Polish was fluent from his many years of Sunday studies, and Billy had little trouble with German; having parents who grew up in the Austro-Hungarian Empire helped. He loved science, but it didn't come as naturally as language and history. This bright boy dreaming of excitement was suited more for gestalt experience than for traditional education.

Textile High had been only two years along when Billy arrived for his first freshman day in 1924. Principal William Henry Dooley was a progressive educator who, after training at Columbia and Harvard Universities, visited garment trade schools in Europe and the high schools of the mill town of Lowell, Massachusetts, before setting up his great experiment: a feeder school for the New York garment industry. There were plenty of employment opportunities for Dooley's well-trained graduates in the robust economy of the 1920s.

Billy dutifully enrolled in interior design classes such as History of Furniture, Color Schemes, and Coherence in Decorating, but he excelled off-curriculum, mastering his own quirky enthusiasms and playing well with others. He studied costume illustration (mandatory for both boys and girls), batik (a dying technique especially popular in Javanese design), and life drawing, where nude models posed for students in the school's exceedingly progressive classrooms. His classmates learned commercial poster design and advertising. And Billy adored his art history elective, especially rule breaker Vincent van Gogh and his friend Paul Gauguin, who painted sensual South Pacific women. Billy loved the racy Gauguins.

He happily took his commute on the Long Island Railroad from the barn-red Bayside train station to Manhattan's Penn Station every day rather than go to school in Bayside with dreamless kids who moaned about dirty, greedy Jews and lazy Negroes. Several of his friends at Textile High were black women who had been elected school leaders, such as Aurie Aileen Carter, an officer in the history and law club who was headed to Pratt Institute, and the class vice president, Florizel Cunningham, who'd been accepted to New York University. Why couldn't those living lusterless lives in Queens grasp there was another way to think?

Sure, Billy appreciated some of the Bayside experience: the nearby Oakland Lake and the public tennis courts one block from his house. He even had a go at the local putting green. But overall, he found the neighborhood provincial and boring, even if his mother had written to her relatives in Poland that it was *glamorous*—that she lived where most of the American silent-film stars lived. (She neglected to mention the actors were in a snootier part of town.)

In the spring of 1927, Billy's first year as a Queens resident and his junior year of high school, Richard Evelyn Byrd lost the Orteig Prize to Charles Lindbergh for being the first to fly nonstop from New York to Paris. (Back in 1919, New York City hotel owner Raymond Orteig had offered a prize of $25,000 for the first nonstop aircraft flight between the two cities.)

Lindbergh was now the most lionized man in America, and Billy was undoubtedly disappointed and razzed about it by friends. His idol had long been Byrd, for years the heavy favorite to win the Orteig—until Lindbergh became an overnight sensation on May 21, 1927, the day he landed his single-engine plane at Paris's Le Bourget Airport. Still, Billy was proud of Byrd when he read about the christening of the commander's newest Fokker trimotor aircraft, designed to cross the Atlantic. In front of a brass band and two thousand admirers at Roosevelt Field, Byrd had been slipped a disturbing note: Lindbergh had beaten him to the punch and made it to Paris in thirty-three and a half hours. The astute commander had nothing but praise that day for the young upstart from the Midwest; knowing that he could no longer win, he announced that he would fly anyway for the experience. Byrd, as Billy saw it, was all class. Nothing set him back, not even public humiliation. He just powered on, in it for the adventure, not the prize.

Of course, Byrd must have been crestfallen. But he had gentlemanly let Lindbergh use Roosevelt Field—a milelong patch of dirt that Byrd had leased personally—as a runway two days before. The beautifully smooth path from which Lindbergh's custom-built Ryan monoplane, the *Spirit of St. Louis,* took off had been leveled especially for the commander.

Mayor James "Jimmy" Walker—friend to celebrity, master logroller—gave Byrd his second tickertape parade in thirteen months for his sporting spirit. The turnout for the runner-up was sparse compared with Lindbergh's record-breaking crowds, and it rained hard that Monday, and many left the July 18 parade early, but no way was Billy missing it: school was out, and he stayed to the bitter end.

By the end of 1927, even though Byrd had been given a Congressional Medal of Honor for his troubles, pesky rumors about Byrd's North Pole 1926 exploits on his Fokker trimotor aircraft *Josephine*

Ford (shrewdly named after patron Edsel Ford's daughter) weren't going away. How could he and his pilot, Floyd Bennett, have made a 1,500-mile return trip in such a short time: fifteen hours and forty-four minutes instead of the expected eighteen hours? Commander Byrd maintained they had been aided by strong tailwinds. But criticism smarted. And after having lost the Orteig to Lindbergh, Byrd longed to solidify his unexpectedly shaky place in history and hankered after everlasting fame. How to get the attention of a jaded America?

He sought the guidance of Edward Bernays, Sigmund Freud's nephew and a trusted advisor who later would be credited as the founder of the public relations field. Bernays had salvaged President Calvin Coolidge's public image during his 1924 campaign, inviting vaudeville stars to a pancake breakfast at the White House in hopes of enticing the notoriously dour politician to crack a smile for the cameras. With Bernays's expert help, Coolidge won the office. Now Bernays brainstormed with Byrd: Why not replace that loss to Lindbergh with a win? Could he fly somewhere dramatic and film it? Americans were still enraptured by flight. A year after his victory, Lucky Lindy was still pictured everywhere holding up his $25,000 Orteig Prize check. He had toured seventy-five American cities in the *Spirit of St. Louis* the previous summer and fall, dropping messages printed on postcards where he couldn't visit. Before 1927, most Americans had been afraid to travel by plane, but Lindbergh's triumph cemented public confidence in flight; investors popped up, and aviation stocks soared. Private airlines surfaced— there were soon forty-four scheduled airlines and as many non-scheduled ones—and by the end of the 1920s, roughly three million Americans, mainly businessmen, had followed Lindbergh across their country's skies.

So, a flight, then. But the North Pole was getting old. What about an expedition to the South Pole that involved airplanes as well as ships?

The Antarctic story to date was wed to European history. Explorers such as England's Shackleton and Norway's Amundsen—and Belgium's Adrien de Gerlache, the first to winter in the region, from March 1898 to March 1899—had captured the fancy of their nations; they'd certainly enjoyed their taste of the sublime. But Americans hadn't particularly followed those expeditions. Byrd understood that Americans needed their own heroes before they'd care. However, to stake his claim to immortality, he needed money. Lots of it. In 1927 the United States government was not in the habit of financing expeditions, a costly business. It was time to hustle, Bernays advised.

Luckily, Byrd was exceptionally good at hustle. Within weeks, he'd written an article in the monthly *World's Work* magazine titled "Why I Am Going to the South Pole," which included the lines "Man cannot claim mastery of the globe until he conquers the Antarctic continent. It is the last great challenge." Here the commander first mentioned his plans to explore from the air, shipping over his planes in a small fleet. Alas, he got carried away during this gestation period. A week later, Byrd "confided" to an already intrigued Associated Press reporter his far-fetched plan not only to take the four best Eskimo hunters out of their blustery rockbound community but also to start a yearlong colony in Antarctica by sending along two squaws to cook their meals and to "breed" more Eskimos. One can only imagine Billy's reaction to this flamboyant update.

Sensationalism and patriotism—those did the trick. The public clamored for more news, any news. Eskimos going to the South Pole! Anything else?

TWO

GOOD MEN
SHOULD APPLY

By February 1928, plans for Commander Byrd's Antarctic expedition were popping up in reputable and disreputable papers alike, although at this stage, the mission was still being followed mostly by science and adventure buffs devouring gossipy reports in somewhat niche publications. Byrd's most loyal fans, like Billy, were informed that male Inuits would indeed be part of the official crew. And Byrd had names: he'd decided to take along Nukaping (who stood just four foot seven and weighed less than 130 pounds) and several other Kalaallisut-speaking Inuits who had proved invaluable to his previous Arctic exploits in northern Greenland's Etah Fjord, so close to the North Pole. "*Etah*," Byrd said, meant "windy place." Even the name of their home, he explained, signaled their expertise; these were men who lived in sealskin tents and hunted caribou, polar bears, walruses, and seals.

Byrd had thought more about "Eskimo duties" near the South Pole, which, as he saw it now, would include handling dog teams, helping his otherwise all-American team transform fifty reindeer skins into Southern Hemisphere survival clothing, and hunting seal to feed the party.

"I don't know how the Eskimos will take to the heat," he joked to a newspaper reporter at the *New York World*. "Maybe I'll have to put the whole lot of them on ice until we reach colder climes."

Over at *Popular Science*, writer "Fitz" Green teased readers with more details. Green was already the explorer's trusted ghostwriter, though this was not disclosed. Green had traveled with Byrd on his North Pole exploits and knew his "Eskimo friend" Nukaping, offering, "He is stockily built, has never had a bath, and prefers raw meat to cooked. The only food he eats regularly besides meat is raw eider duck eggs." How would he fare so far from the windy place he called home? Green quoted Byrd: "Nukaping will not realize that we are going to the southern end of the globe. He'll think he is back home when he sees the ice and snow again."

Someone as canny as PR strategist Bernays was pulling strings as enthralling plans (not all of them plausible) continued to leak out. Small newswire pieces and science magazine scoops would help amass crowds for a profitable fund-raising lecture-circuit trip around the nation.

Then, on March 11, 1928, premier aviation reporter Russell Owen announced the whole game in the *New York Times*. Owen was an unlikely adventurer. Three years earlier, the bespectacled thirty-six-year-old had covered the Scopes trial—a national victory for science, when a high school substitute teacher named John T. Scopes was exonerated for violating Tennessee's Butler Act, which outlawed the teaching of human evolution in public schools. After his exemplary coverage, Owen had more say in his assignments and won the right to cover Byrd's 1926 North Pole trip, flying as far as Ny-Ålesund, on the Norwegian Arctic Ocean archipelago of Svalbard, where he met and interviewed Byrd. With that relationship in place, Owen had been a natural choice to cover the 1927 Lindbergh-Byrd race. The navy commander had been thrilled to give Owen the scoop and privately asked the *Times* to later send Owen along on his Antarctica voyage, where he could cover the flight over the South Pole. Still, the *New York Times* paid good money for Russell Owen's access to Byrd.

Reclining in an easy chair in the governor's mansion in Richmond, Virginia, Byrd formally revealed his plans. He and Owen were there at the invitation of Byrd's older brother, Harry, who had been elected the state's governor two years before—the latest in a long line of Byrd overachievers. Richard Byrd's base of operations was a lackluster room in the Hotel McAlpin in New York's Herald Square; perhaps Harry's new mansion was a more impressive backdrop for this interview and would reinforce the luster of the Byrd name.

As for the specific details divulged: "On the final dash for the pole," the *Times* reported, "we shall carry a Primus stove, a reindeer sleeping bag, two months' food supply, including Danish-made pemmican (a highly caloric emergency ration), chocolate, tea, hardtack, and dog food. We will also have skis, snowshoes, medical kits, extra clothing, and rifles and ammunition." With this much thought having gone into preparations, the expedition would surely be under way soon.

As a longtime Byrd devotee, Billy's ears pricked up whenever he heard new press dispatches on the American South Pole trip. Owen's scoop was cut and pasted into his scrapbook, a craft he'd learned from his mother. Photos of Billy, like the clippings from his pet show win, featured prominently in hers, but his was devoted solely to the expedition. Clipping news for it was the most exciting part of his day. Otherwise, like any restless senior, Billy trudged through his final year at Textile High.

The *Times* soon ran almost daily stories about "America's Explorer." Bravery was a constant theme, and Commander Byrd was often photographed in his full-dress white uniform, which he had obtained permission from the US Navy to wear. In truth, he fared only moderately well in the navy, exiting as a junior-grade lieutenant after having sustained a personal injury outside the line of duty. Although acquaintances knew that his fine charm masked a huge ego (and an even more select few knew that he possessed dodgy flying skills), nothing disparaging about Byrd was considered fair copy—even from the *Times*'s rivals, which had begun to cover the growing story, too.

The newsmen of Owen's generation were invested in making their countrymen proud. Even after World War I, America was still widely regarded as something of an upstart country, with Europe considered the height of sophistication. Now here was a man who conveyed an unimpeachable high-WASP elegance: a handsome, slender figure with a shock of black hair, a delicate nose, eyes ringed with dark, long lashes, a square jawline, and an "Old Dominion" Virginian refined demeanor. If a risk taker, Byrd was a genteel one: curious, focused, gracious to his competitors, a dog lover, and in it for something larger than the prize. He was a homegrown hero who might inspire jealousy from even the old-boys-club Europeans emulated by the American wannabes.

Not that Byrd was getting all the attention—the unexplored expanses of Antarctica intrigued readers, too. At night, after finishing homework, Billy swooned at electrifying rumors that there could be unknown creatures in its uncharted lands. He pasted these reports into his scrapbook too, among them one particularly stirring quote attributed to Byrd in a February 1928 *Popular Mechanics* article:

> "Does it seem reasonable that lands which for months of the year are swept by sunshine twenty-four hours a day should not somewhere support life? Not on the great plateaus which stretch out inland to the pole; here there is only snow and ice. But somewhere in those tremendous areas there must be low-lands where temperatures rise sufficiently to permit vegetable and animal life—the latter very possibly as different from any we know as the penguin is different from birds of climes with which we are familiar.
>
> "In some antarctic [*sic*] valley, perhaps, shut in by towering mountains, a thrilling discovery awaits us. We may find forms of life completely new to us. Who knows what link with prehistoric times might be there?"

By the time of the first major *New York Times* story on Byrd's expedition that March, forty thousand people had applied to go to Antarctica without knowing what position they might be assigned, or even if the expedition would accept applications. Even Byrd was surprised by how many were ready to work for free in a decade when fast-growing companies with increasing demand for labor paid respectable wages of $20 a week, good enough for a room in a boarding house. (A real striver could earn triple that.) Within a day of Russell Owen's article, applications began pouring in by the sackful. There was still no rundown of which spots were available—some, surely, would be filled by people Byrd already knew—or which skills were necessary to apply. Byrd's people severely underestimated the number of applications that would end up on their desks to sort through; between twenty thousand and forty thousand wishful letters—some papers claimed the number was closer to sixty thousand—arrived at the makeshift office in the Hotel McAlpin.

Byrd picked his staff in great secrecy. Members of the Rockefeller and Vanderbilt clans were among the thousands who competed for spots and were rejected even as mess boys. Following the commander's wishes, staffers avoided taking on too many rich grandstanders. There were some, sure—he had favors to return—but Byrd also handpicked a microcosm of America from its population of 110 million: plenty of Swedes, Scots, Irish, Italians, and even a Jew. But not, Billy noted, a single Pole. Maybe that would be his in, if he applied. There was no deadline; applications were rolling, answered if a man like that was needed. He'd need a guardian's approval, though: he was still seventeen, with his eighteenth birthday, so frustratingly, on September 10, days after the volunteers would set sail. If only his pop would sign that damn parental waiver!

Owen soon revealed that Byrd's advisor on the expedition was none other than fifty-six-year-old Roald Amundsen, the Norwegian who had reached the South Pole first. The two explorers had met in person at least once in Spitsbergen, Norway, on the island of Svalbard, when Amundsen was photographed offering congratulations after Byrd's "successful" flight over the North Pole. The two egoists had come to like each other, exchanging letters over the past months. Amundsen, who had been first mate of the unprecedented "overwintering" at Antarctica (on Adrien de Gerlache's trapped ship *Belgica*, in 1898 and 1899), was the world's most experienced living explorer, and it was for his familiarity with the polar region that Byrd listened to him the most. He warned Byrd of the changeable nature of Antarctic ice: that one year it could be everywhere and the next year nowhere at all. Steely eyed and efficient, Amundsen had taken a risk in wintering on the Ross Ice Barrier in 1911, understanding that ice could break off, or calve, and plunge his primitive polar colony into disaster, but he wasn't wrong. And he'd beaten Scott to the pole, hadn't he? Amundsen, always careful in assessing the competition, knew Byrd couldn't pilot a plane that well, but he thought the commander shared his combination of caution and guts—as Amundsen saw it, unusual in a glut of rash explorers—and the American was an excellent navigator, a skill not to be knocked. Amundsen knew his old pedestrian-and-dogsled methods were almost obsolete; he understood as well as Byrd that aviation was the way of modern exploration. Powered flight would put the final pieces of the jigsaw in place.

The pragmatic Norwegian suggested the flagship for Byrd's Antarctica expedition: a Scandinavian ship called *Samson*, made for hunting seals in icy conditions. He knew the boat well, having worked on it in the Arctic as a younger man. The forty-six-year-old ship was a windjammer: 161 feet long, 27 feet across at the beam, and wooden sides 34 inches thick, to withstand the shock of breaking through ice. Byrd ran the idea past William Todd, a very prominent businessman friend who owned a shipping yard in New York, one of the largest in the country. Todd helped locate the old vessel in Tromsø, Norway, and offered to convert it to a barque (short for "barquentine"): a romantic type of ship with three or more masts. The barque would be almost archaic, evocative of the grand old days; for instance, Ernest Shackleton's legendary *Endurance* had been a barque that got trapped in the Antarctic ice and was crushed. Bernays wasn't Byrd's only friend with a knack for PR.

After speaking with Byrd, Owen reported, Todd arranged for the sealer to sail to his Brooklyn yards via Oslo. She arrived following two months at sea, with rotted sails and rigging, ready for rebirth.

So even the famous Amundsen shared his admiration for Byrd! How Billy yearned for a taste of dangers, hardships, thrills on the ice. He pestered his father yet again for a chance to apply, but Rudy told Billy sternly to pick up his uneven grades so that he might have a shot at the prestigious Cooper Union arts course: the revered institution in downtown Manhattan offered free tuition for those who deserved the chance. Many of Billy's teachers considered him a bright fantasist and worried about his chronic absenteeism, even if he passed tests well enough to graduate. They warned his parents that life required focus; big dreams were never enough.

If most of Billy's fellow students were not attending the elite Ivies because of financial hardship—not to mention prejudicial quotas against Jews, Italians, and African Americans—they were on track to receive offers from places such as the free City College system located between West 130th and West 141st Streets in Manhattan. America's first municipal university filled quickly with young men and women from the immigrant Jewish community in particular. In a mere thirty years, college enrollment had tripled, with female, minority, and immigrant enrollment drummed up by suffragists and educational reformers. Still, Rudy often joked with his wife that what their underperforming kid really needed wasn't college but a kick up the backside. What an advantage he had over his parents in life! Work harder! Stop talking about Antarctica! Billy did work harder—on learning more about the expedition.

Floyd Bennett was dead. Billy couldn't believe it. He had read that Bennett was the steadiest of pilots, always putting caution before thrill. Bennett had met Richard Byrd back in 1918 in flight school in Pensacola, Florida. While Bennett was not dynamic—a little on the dull side for an aviator—Byrd, who valued loyalty above any character trait, had come to consider him his closest friend. How could the thirty-seven-year-old man who piloted Byrd to the North Pole and shared his 1926 tickertape parade be dead of pneumonia? Would the expedition to Antarctica continue?

Byrd, reporters said, was visibly shaken at the burial in Arlington

National Cemetery on April 27, 1928. The tragedy had made him question whether he had it in him to go through with his plans. But his friend would want him to keep going, he decided. After the funeral, he pulled a stone from Bennett's grave to carry with him and drop over the South Pole when the time came. To the press attending the funeral, he explained that after an emotional graveside chat with his old friend, he would continue with a spirit of noblesse oblige.

A few days later, when back in New York City, Byrd confirmed his decision to press on during a press conference in the teaky Biltmore Hotel, where, in suite 340, a half dozen secretaries and a telephone switchboard operator worked at high speed. After Byrd's embarrassing one-room suite at the Hotel McAlpin, he'd next arranged a move to the Putnam offices at 2 West Forty-Fifth Street. The rooms were provided by his publisher, George "Gyp" Putnam (grandson of the founder of G. P. Putnam's Sons), friend of the daring flyboys and an explorer himself: in 1926 the American Museum of Natural History had sponsored Putnam's Arctic expedition, and in 1927—the year he published Charles Lindbergh's *We*, the most successful nonfiction book to date—he had led an expedition for the American Geographical Society to collect specimens on Baffin Island in the Arctic Ocean of northernmost Canada.

But in Byrd's private view, the Putnam Building was still not impressive enough for a commander. He networked with fellow horse lover John McEntee Bowman, the new owner of the Biltmore, who offered him living quarters and office space on the third floor. Byrd accepted happily. The Biltmore was a luxurious hotel next to Grand Central Station, significant enough to have played host to President Woodrow Wilson and Sherlock Holmes creator Sir Arthur Conan Doyle, and complete with its own private train track. Byrd knew his time there would coincide with that of former New York governor Al Smith, who was on another floor planning the Empire

State Building, his second act after having lost the 1928 presidential election to Republican Herbert Hoover. Byrd and Smith knew one another through friends and often asked after each other's highly publicized progress in the Biltmore's elevators and lobby.

With the warmth of spring and the pangs of love that went with the season, Billy had his first steady girlfriend in 1928. This dark-haired beauty was edgier than the flossy flappers with their daddies' money. She never teased him that his voice had not deepened fully or that his immigrant heritage was a deal breaker—that was her ancestry, too. She went to his arty public high school, after all: a street-smart, down-to-earth, regular New Yorker like him, zippy and talented and burning to make her mark. They posed for photos together, a dyad of bohemians. (If only he had written his darling's name on the back of those photographs!)

Impulsive as Billy was, almost as soon as he met this good-looking gal, he started with the I-love-yous. Weeks later, he wanted to marry her. He and his girl had been together for a solid two months now. How was this a lark? But his pop would have none of this nonsense. Why did he risk coming to America? Did Rudy have to remind Billy that he would inherit his interior decoration business one day? His son needed to be sensible, go to college, and master a trade. Rudy had built up a clientele that admired him—some of them, as he had hoped, now lower-tier silent-movie stars, for he was a handsome and personable self-educated man with a sense for elegance.

Francesca begged Billy to stop his folly, and this time when his father yelled at him in fury, Billy obeyed. He was a kid; he wasn't willing to lose his parents. But he did not break up with The One right away, not before the Textile High prom. That would have been cruel to both of them.

Billy's senior prom started Friday, May 4, at eight thirty, in the big dance hall at the Waldorf-Astoria Hotel, with music by the Dick Stiles Orchestra. It was a relief to not enter the floor as a stag begging for a dance. This was one of the last proms at the old Waldorf, a lavish hotel on Fifth Avenue and Thirty-Fourth Street that would soon be demolished to make way for the Empire State Building. But that May night, the hall was bathed in fragrance, with flowers at every table and girls in evening gowns with flowers pinned in their hair gliding over the dance floor with their escorts, each, like Billy, wearing a boutonnière. The student newspaper the *Textilian*'s final issue for the year called the evening perfect down to the last waltz.

The best-paid people on Richard Byrd's staff were press agents, and others gave him PR advice for free. Publisher Gyp Putnam pushed the commander to run a contest to select a scout to join the crew. A true-life account of the journey to Antarctica by an American Boy Scout might be a bestseller. Byrd considered Putnam a fellow who knew how to market adventure even better than he did—and Byrd had taken Harvard Business School classes in marketing to prepare for the expedition. Gyp Putnam was certainly onto something: Ernest Shackleton had launched his own contest eight years earlier, choosing James Marr from 1,500 British applicants to join the 1921 Quest expedition. The eighteen-year-old Scot went on to write *Into the Frozen South*, a book for boys like Billy, captivated by polar journeys. He had a lot to write about, as Shackleton never even made it to Antarctica, dying of a heart attack on barren South Georgia Island in the South Atlantic.

Byrd would have his own Boy Scout. The sensational contest was announced in June. And if all 826,000 Boys Scouts had wanted to go on Byrd's trip, 80,000 of them immediately applied from across America.

In Billy Gawronski's final days at Textile High, the crash of the airship *Italia* during a flight around the North Pole, and the rising career of a beguiling young aviatrix named Amelia Earhart dominated headlines. The kidnapping of a ten-year-old New York City girl named Grace Budd was much spoken of, too. (A few years later, this crime would be linked to infamous serial cannibal Albert Fish— Grace was eaten.) But the Textile seniors of 1928 were less concerned with the front-page news than with the dreaded New York State Regents Exam that commenced Monday, June 18, and lasted all week. This was considered their final exam. But even while studying, Billy was reminded of Byrd: a New York dairy firm had bought the right to produce official expedition protective covers, distributed free to all students, with which he had covered his books.

After getting their passing marks, the seniors would be free. But Billy knew he wouldn't be, not really, not from his father; he was still scheming about how to get Rudy to sign his parental release papers for the heartfelt application he planned to send Byrd. He could be a low-level seaman, ordered to stand watch at the crow's nest or maybe even to take a trick at the wheel. Anything he could do for Commander Byrd would be an honor.

Then came the second death. On June 18, the first day of the Regents Exam, Roald Amundsen, that hypervigilant first man to reach the South Pole, disappeared with five others during a rescue mission to find the airship already in the news, the *Italia*, which had crashed near the North Pole. Their bodies would never be found. It was another setback for Byrd: a lost advisor on the heels of the death of his pilot and dear friend. And to think that Amundsen had once been a rival, back when Byrd snatched from him the first flight over the North Pole in 1926.

Yes, it was a tragic coda to the Norwegian's career, but at least Amundsen had died a death befitting an explorer. Many had perished magnificently in the Antarctic, including Ernest Shackleton and much of Robert Falcon Scott's party, who froze and starved to death in 1912 when their supplies ran out. Who would die in Byrd's expedition? In a perverse way, the fear—the very real fear—added to the appeal. Billy knew Scott's last words (found in his diary) by heart: "Had we lived, I should have had a tale to tell of the hardihood, endurance, and courage of my companions that would have stirred the heart of every Englishman. These rough notes and our bodies must tell the tale."

Again the teenager decided to make a last-minute plea for sending a Pole to the pole. But again and again, Rudy Gawronski waved away the paperwork Billy desperately typed out for him.

Rudy had his own idols. His pet quote was from the Polish general Józef Piłsudski, a hero of the Great War and, to many proud Polish men, their country's George Washington: "To be defeated and yet not surrender, this is victory." He made Billy say the words out loud: *"Byc zwyciezonym I nie ulec to zwyciestwo."* How Rudy wished his son worshipped the truly brave Piłsudski more than this manufactured hero Byrd.

Byrdmania wasn't just for boys and men. Among the rush of letters from around the world were hundreds of applications from women and girls spurred on by high-profile achievements of adventurous ladies in their modern era. That very June, Amelia Earhart had become the first woman to fly across the Atlantic as a passenger, while the year before, seventeen-year-old Elinor Smith became the youngest licensed pilot in America. The Long Islander, nicknamed "the Flying Flapper of Freeport," would set a new world altitude record in 1930. Female swimmers were in the news just as frequently: in 1926 Gertrude Ederle, a twenty-year-old Manhattanite whose father was a butcher over by Tenth Avenue, became the first woman to swim the English Channel. Ederle had been given her own parade down

Manhattan's Canyon of Heroes (the stretch of lower Broadway that bisects the financial district); she even made a guest appearance in the now-lost silent romantic comedy *Swim Girl, Swim.*

Miss S. Nevin Wemple, thirty-four, a rare female doctor of dental surgery, of 542 Fifth Avenue, wanted to join Byrd's men as expedition dentist and begged for no publicity. Ann Pender, twenty-three, and Marie Buma, twenty-six, from Worcester, Massachusetts, applied together, writing, "We do not wish for you to get the impression that we are of the flapper type." Winnifred Webster Harlow, a New York consulting character analyst and psychologist, asked for the privilege of accompanying the group as the expedition analyst, explaining, "While each man is studying the pole, I may study the soul. I know my findings would be of interest and help to science." She included a clipping she'd written for the daily tabloid *New York Evening Graphic*, a salacious publication nicknamed the "Porno-Graphic" by the other big dailies. The *Graphic* often used retouched photo collages called Composographs to create "photographs" of events of which it could not obtain actual photos; one such Composograph accompanied Winnifred Harlow's application. The "photo" showed how aviators like Richard Byrd were on track to develop birdlike eyes.

Perhaps the most appealing letter of all came from thirteen-year-old Nancy Pugh from Springville, Louisiana, daughter of Mrs. Nicholls Pugh, who impishly crossed out her mother's name on her stationery and wrote in her own. Her two-page plea ended:

> I'm a tomboy girl. If I were a boy I'd give my eyeteeth to be on one of your expeditions, and I intend to be an adventurer and aviatrix when I am grown. I refuse to stay at home . . . but my mother and daddy have discouraged such work projects. Tell me anyway if I can go in I'll be there. I'm home I wear knickers and

I can do anything any boy can besides being a pretty good shot.
At inanimate things.

Byrd loved her letter and replied via his male secretary, Charley Lofgren, a navy veteran whom he had asked to come on the expedition as his yeoman, for administrative duties: "Won't you please send me your photograph . . . for I greatly admire your pluck?" There was, however, no place on the expedition for little girls.

Even the most accomplished women had little chance of being selected, a fact that New York tabloid journalist and author Delos W. Lovelace (who wrote the novelization of the 1933 movie *King Kong*) made inescapably clear in syndicated papers:

> You would have thought the women could not have failed to see that there was no place for even one of them in such a party as was being organized. What woman could have withstood the rough life, the cold, the rigors of the Antarctic . . . No, we can't use a dishwasher. Our dishwashers must be six feet tall and be able to lick their weight in icebergs if not in wildcats. Mending? Madam, we'll do our own mending or wear 'em ripped. Oh, you are as strong as a man, are you? And used to all sorts of hardships? Went hiking for a full month in Yellowstone Park last summer, did you? Well, even at that we haven't any place. Awfully sorry.

When was Billy's last kiss imprinted upon his girlfriend's cheek? Likely they ended their adolescent love affair in tears near graduation in June. Nevertheless, that painful break set him free to fixate on adventure instead, and pent-up resentment against parental control became additional motivation to get away from his father—and from Bayside.

During his last days of twelfth grade, Billy tried to appear up-beat. He had been accepted to City College, the college for the aspiring masses, and was still waiting to hear from the elite Cooper Union. He didn't mention to friends that his father had "spoken to someone" there—even the immigrant class relied on connections. (His pop's someone was almost always a swimming buddy from the Polish Falcons.) Billy's teachers were making queries, too. He was not Textile's number one student, but they really liked the kid. He was high energy—enthusiastic—and he had a wonderful, memorable smile. Billy half listened to reports on their progress. Cooper Union was his father's priority, not his.

A few days after the last school bell rang, Billy headed for the June 26 graduation ceremony at City College's borrowed Harlem auditorium; his parents and grandmother attended with pride. Upon entry, seniors who paid their fee were issued a copy of the yearbook, *The Loom*. Some thoughts from Principal Dooley were printed on the front page, ending with this advice: "The question may be asked what are the characteristics or qualities that make for leadership . . . The most prominent qualities for leadership are a) character b) personality c) efficiency." Not listed were the two traits most striking in Billy: a taste for adventure, and an openness to new people and things.

Billy turned to his page:

WILLIAM GAWRONSKI
The Medical Society, The Chemistry Club, and
The American History and Law Club

"He wishes he had the charm of his own white rats."

The smart aleck assigned to yearbook captions had an easy quip to write, for the dreary winter day Billy had taken his rats to school was the stuff of legend. Girls had screamed as he raced several rats down the hall with his friends.

After his family left, Billy hung around, gathering signatures in his yearbook and his brown leather autograph book. Principal Dooley liked Billy well enough to sign his name, as did almost all of his teachers, who left cheerful notes. And the genial boy's yearbook brimmed with well-wishes from fellow graduates. The Jewish contingent had no problem with this open-minded Polish Catholic: his yearbook was signed by Isaac Bernstein, a nerdy-looking fellow active in the Menorah Society, and by swarthy swim-club president "Happy" Epstein, whose own caption read: "Who refuses to swim the English Channel; claims it is too effeminate." There was a long, hearty send-off from the president of the senior class, Nathan Budnitz—also voted Most Popular Boy. Then there were the Italians, including the Best Looking Boy, Attilio Tadde, who was off to Princeton University. "Take care," scribbled Gennaro Fanelli, "the Dancing Wizard of 1928." "Best wishes!" wrote Silvio Fressola, "the Don Juan of Greenwich Village."

Billy's former girlfriend had dark hair and eyes. Was she in a lower grade? She certainly was not blond looker Gladys Lloyd, vice president of the class, who had been accepted to Syracuse University upstate and wrote "Best wishes!" Was she brunette Gertrude Dickstein, the one who wrote the eyebrow-raising "Goodbye from your *sax* teacher"? Or could she have been Jewish Ruth Dvoren, voted "Best Looking Girl" and indeed lushly pretty on the page—very pale, with thick black hair and searing eyes. Dvoren wrote a "perhaps" note: "Lots of luck for—*always*."

Much as they liked the boy, Billy's friends didn't get his obsession with Antarctica. Why couldn't he admit that his chances of getting his father's permission to apply had gotten worryingly thin? Yes, it was an irritation to give in to parental pressure, but what did he think he would do with his life beyond help his father? That was an easy, safe path for him, all could agree.

Did Billy know he was in the same boat that the missing Roald Amundsen was once in? Not many things in the world frightened Amundsen, except his mother, who had insisted he go to medical school. For a time, Amundsen had listened and was an exemplary student in everything but medicine. He was freed for a life of adventure only when his mother died unexpectedly in 1893, at which point, he dropped out of university. Had she lived to a ripe old age, somewhere in Oslo there might have been a frustrated doctor, and Robert Scott might have been first to the pole.

The only one in Billy's family who wanted him to chase his passions was his dear old babcia. His foreign-born aunts and uncles who had settled in America—following Rudy first to the Lower East Side and then out to Queens—were baffled by his polar fixation. So were his cousins, and they'd grown up as Americans. Only Babcia shared his wild beliefs in his future. One day in July she gave him her special spiritual charm engraved with the words "Sacred Heart of Jesus I Place My Trust in Thee." He wore it around his neck that summer, even in the water, and would wear it on all of his later journeys. (Billy would carry a creased photo of his beloved babcia in each brown calfskin wallet he owned throughout the years.)

Another day that summer, Billy was called to his grandmother's half-story attic bedroom, where she stared at him with her age-beaten eyes. His babcia had seen something *vonderful* in the shiny ball she brought with her to Bayside along with her many amulets to ward off the evil eye: Billy would be with Richard E. Byrd, she insisted. Her grandson laughed. At least she was trying to cheer him up. She loved him.

However, Billy's mother had had it with Babcia's big talk and demanded that her husband tell his mother to stop the unnecessary encouragement. Francesca's weekly letters to her own mother in Poland were written on postcards and filmy airmail stationery in Kurrent, the Gothic medieval form of German that many Poles in the Austro-Hungarian Empire had been taught to write before the Great War. The letters detailed Rudy's growing business and Billy's not-so-amusing preoccupation with Commander Byrd. In smaller handwriting, a careful reader of Kurrent (and there are not many left) will find mention of Francesca's conflicts with her mother-in-law.

Graduation behind him, Billy joined Rudy on client calls and assisted his color-blind father in picking out fabrics. Only Billy and Francesca knew his father's secret shame: how in the privacy of their home, Billy described and suggested suitable hues. A few months earlier, Rudy had Americanized the family's last name to Gavron—but for business only; nothing official with the government. He encouraged his son to do his part and give the wealthy of Bayside a card if he met them on the Long Island Railroad or the tennis courts; he was *always* to remember that he would inherit the upholstery business.

Angry with his parents, yet expected to help his father, Billy was without a girlfriend that summer, not to mention hot and miserable—rare was a house with air-conditioning in those days. He didn't even want to help Babcia in the garden, where she grew potatoes and cabbage and sunflowers that would soon be tall enough to be photographed by Rudy for the family photo album.

Then his mood changed.

Of all people, Commander Richard Byrd was moving to Bayside. Billy read the incredible news on July 13, 1928, in a local Queens publication, the *Daily Star*. Seeking relief from humidity and intensifying intrusion into his privacy, the paper explained, thirty-nine-year-old Richard Byrd and his wife, Marie, had decided to move their four young children from their apartment in sweltering Manhattan's luxurious but cramped Biltmore Hotel to the lush Bayside Avenue home of sixty-five-year-old performer Andrew Mack, who was summering elsewhere and happy to rent them his home. Not only would the newsworthy couple gain privacy, but now Byrd would be closer to the planes he'd fly over the South Pole—both being serviced in Uniondale, Long Island, east and south of Bayside near Roosevelt Field—and could supervise their maintenance on a more regular basis.

Andrew Mack was a multitalented man, a vaudevillian comedian and legitimate stage actor who composed "The Story of a Rose," a barbershop quartet standard and popular Valentine's Day tune that would remain so even a hundred years later. Mack's house on Little Neck Bay was close to the water, and his landscaped grounds were heavily scented with roses and gardenia tended to by a private gardener.

Byrd's imminent arrival in Bayside was the lucky break Billy had prayed for. He could "bump" into Byrd and pitch him personally. Billy now looked both ways for his hero every time he left the house. Francesca frowned when she spied this from the window. Enough already: she expected her son to help with housework and get past his adolescent fantasies.

The commander would sail in September, the latest news reports said, seeing his flagship off past the Statue of Liberty and returning to shore by tug as his men continued to New Zealand. Byrd would then set sail later, leaving California in more comfort aboard the whaler *C. A. Larsen*. The local press also reported that the commander hobnobbed daily with all those fancy folk over at Actors Row and that the expedition was still $300,000 short. Perhaps Byrd had an ulterior motive for moving to the rich enclave.

Every grueling August day, the commander had something big planned. In an address to the well-salaried industry fellows of the

Advertising Club of New York broadcast on local radio, Byrd announced he was honoring his host city by renaming his flagship. The *Samson* would now be called the *City of New York*.

One day, at the beginning of the month, Billy caught sight of Byrd on Bayside's main street, Bell Boulevard. He thrilled at seeing him away from the chaos of tickertape parades, but his chest thumped so loudly that he couldn't dare approach. Still, he took this unexpected sighting as an auspicious sign.

After seeing Byrd on his own turf, Billy braved his luck and pressed his father again about permission to apply. Rudy stared. Was his son botched in the head? Rudy read the papers, too. He knew that some of the wealthiest men in the nation had applied for unglamorous jobs as sailmakers, carpenters, mechanics, oilers, and cooks. Harvard boys would scrub bottles to get a crack at adventure. Couldn't Billy get that in his skull? Sons of the superpowerful going as bottle scrubbers! Anyone would hoot at an application by a first-generation immigrant's kid. "The only people who will look after Poles," he told his son, "are other Poles!"

Billy fought back as best as he could without getting a lashing. What about Rudy's good relationships with his Jewish suppliers and his Protestant Bayside customers? This was the modern day! This was *America*. But the parental consent form remained unsigned.

A week into August, Cooper Union accepted Billy into its interior design program, all expenses paid. His parents were jubilant. Francesca jabbered away at the remaining Polish summer social events, dragging her son along.

But every bitter day, Billy read about the latest applicants accepted for Byrd's expedition. Six national finalists for the Boy Scout contest had emerged, all Eagle Scouts. They would gather in New York for Byrd to decide whom he liked best, with the front-runners living together until there was a victor. When they arrived in

mid-August, a wire service photographer brought them to the Gowanus, Brooklyn, shipyard where the flagship was being fixed up and
asked the candidates to wave and smile. And they did, holding on
from various parts of the mast.

In Queens, Billy looked at each face. Who would it be? Even if
he applied for any task at this late date—scrubbing toilets, slicing
potatoes—even if his father signed the waiver, how the hell would a
boy like him wangle a spot? That was as likely as a flapper dating
a newsboy. He had no experience except assisting his father with
upholstery clients and occasionally lighting stoves on Friday nights
for his Jewish friends' families. Byrd wasn't going to hire a *Shabbos*
goy over a scientist.

Byrd's staff continued to evaluate the Boy Scouts over luncheons
and administered the US Army Alpha intelligence test. The young
men were drilled in stenography, a skill that Byrd though might
prove useful on the journey. He might need an extra secretary.

Beat reporters said a favorite had emerged: Paul Siple, a nineteen-
year-old Eagle Scout from Erie, Pennsylvania, who had whomped
his competition with a dumbfounding fifty-nine (out of eighty-eight)
merit badges, the most of any Boy Scout in the nation. His badges included astronomy, aviation, blacksmithing, carpentry, conservation,
electricity, handicraft, hiking, interpreting, journalism, leatherwork,
machinery, painting, pathfinding, photography, physical develop-
ment, pioneering, plumbing, radio, seamanship, signaling, stalking,
surveying, and taxidermy. According to reports, he already had "five
years of experience as a Sea Scout and had spent thirty-five weeks in
total under canvas, including four weeks' winter camping in snow
conditions, often by himself." Every child in America who had fanta-
sized about taking the trip to the South Pole soon knew Paul Siple's
name.

Siple was the epitome of wholesome: white, Protestant, well

mannered, and eager to please. What a bonus, to have scientific and survival chops. Fifty-nine badges and a dutiful smile clinched the spot: before reporters with cameras, Byrd signed Siple on as an orderly.

This was Billy's dream! Paul Siple was living *his* dream!

When he stopped by his old neighborhood to play some summer stickball, his friends laughed at how he rattled off the men on the crew list published in the *New York Times* as well as they could the Brooklyn Dodgers' roster. Martin Ronne, he was the oldest, Billy explained, and the only one to have been in Antarctica before. He was a tailor and tent maker who had overwintered in minus-60-degree-Fahrenheit weather at the secret camp Amundsen set up on the ice barrier to beat Robert Scott's British party to the geographic South Pole. Didn't his friends understand that this man had been at Framheim base with Amundsen? Then there was James Feury from Patterson, New Jersey, a twenty-eight-year-old who had gone with Byrd to the North Pole. Billy's friends did at least know the name of thirty-six-year-old airplane mechanic Benjamin Roth, raised like them on the Lower East Side, on Avenue A. He would be the first Jew to go to Antarctica. He was even bringing his prayer shawl, the Jewish papers reported.

Seventeen veterans of Byrd's 1926 North Pole expedition would be along for the new journey, and twenty-five navy men, with the army and marines represented, too. Legendary dog trainer Arthur Walden would also be on board; for all his expedition's modernity, Byrd was relying on dogsleds as backup, on Amundsen's advice. Walden had been a dog musher in northwest Canada two years before the Klondike gold rush of 1898. Byrd's PR people had hired Walden a ghostwriter and had an autobiography out before the expedition began, and by August, *A Dog Puncher on the Yukon* was a bestseller. Walden's real-life story was as exciting to Billy as any adventure novel by Jack London. A Yukon dog puncher who; by his own admission, had never been south of Philadelphia? If Walden could only sit down for a meal with him on Antarctic ice . . .

Only two weeks before the first ship was due to depart, Billy met one of the expedition members at a well-promoted meet and greet at Gimbel Brothers department store's music department, where, on Thirty-Third Street and Sixth Avenue, a seaman named Richard "Ukulele Dick" Konter played his ukulele and talked about the expedition. He was learning Mammy songs, he said, for the Maoris in New Zealand and the unknown native peoples they would perhaps meet in Antarctica. (Mammy songs are stereotypical tunes about matronly black women that would be offensive to modern ears.) In his prior experience near the North Pole, he explained, classical music did nothing for "simpleminded natives"—just jazz. He then played the crowd "That's My Mammy," a popular song about black women tending the white children of the South. (When the crew reached New Zealand, Konter would play hundreds of Maoris "Alabama Mammy" before popping off to Antarctica, where, of course, there would never be any indigenous peoples for him to meet.)

That August, a new dance caught on called the Byrd Hop. According to (confusing) written accounts, the steps involved takeoff, flight, and landing. Likely it was not as much of a fad as the Lindy Hop, named after Lindbergh's "hop" across the ocean, but it did get good press coverage.

Those less on-trend could read in the papers about Byrd's detailed plans for the twelve-thousand-mile, three-month journey south. His armada would consist of four ships: the renamed flagship the *City of New York*, the supply ship the *Chelsea*, and two giant whalers, the *C. A. Larsen* and the *Sir James Clark Ross*. The latter two would go only as far as Dunedin, New Zealand, where the dogs and planes they had carried would be transferred to the two smaller ships. Some of the men would be left in New Zealand, too; only the luckiest would overwinter on the Antarctic ice.

Three of Byrd's ships would begin their journey from the East Coast: the *New York*, from Hoboken on August 25; the *Chelsea*, from Brooklyn on September 16; and the *Ross*, from Norfolk, Virginia, around the same time that month. The *Larsen*, which would push off from Los Angeles, would not leave for the Southern Hemisphere until October.

Byrd would travel on the *Larsen* along with the two planes and a shortwave radio with a wavelength of 32.5 meters that could test the geographical limits of the new technology. He hoped to prove the device—first used for long-distance transmissions only earlier in the decade—capable of communicating with a station in Bergen, Norway, fourteen thousand miles away. A special corded telephone would also be on board for Byrd's use—a modern device that Shackleton and Scott surely could have used on their doomed voyages.

The *Sir James Clark Ross* was named after the first great Antarctic explorer back in the early nineteenth century: the handsomest man in the British Royal Navy and a daring man at sea from the age of twelve. (Ross also gave his name to Byrd's destination, the Ross Sea.) The fastest and largest ship in Byrd's flotilla—Norwegian built, too; it was impossible to find a good polar expedition ship built in America—the *Ross* would transport the cold-weather expedition dogs (and forty tons of dog biscuits) so that the valuable canines would arrive in good health, getting to New Zealand before almost all the men. The ninety-seven dogs had been handpicked in Canada's remote Newfoundland and Labrador Province by the veterinarian who tended to President Hoover's Belgian shepherd, King Tut.

The cargo steamer the *Chelsea* had been purchased at the last minute; Byrd needed more space for supplies. His expedition office paid only $34,000, a bargain, as the ship had been seized as a rumrunner, bringing illicit alcohol from the Caribbean to American shores. These were the days of Prohibition.

The three ships departing from the East Coast would pass through Cristóbal, the port city on the Atlantic side of the Panama Canal. They would reach the Pacific Ocean via the canal in a few days' time and then, sometime in October, would pass a smattering of islands off the coast of South America. (This would include the Galápagos, where in the 1830s Charles Darwin studied the peculiar isolated animals that led to his theory of evolution.) Then it was on to Tahiti: Billy could only imagine what *that* would be like. He had ogled those sensual Gauguin reproductions of exotic women, exposed. After the interlude of broiling South Pacific sun, the fleet (now accompanied by the *Larsen*) would travel another three thousand miles to New Zealand to refuel and then navigate in dropping temperatures to what reporters on the Byrd beat called the Eighth Wonder of the World: the Ross Ice Barrier (now called the Ross Ice Shelf), and according to the *New York Times*, "a great table-land of solid ice, two-hundred or more feet high" and nearly the size of France. An explorer might as well try to sail through the White Cliffs of Dover.

Roald Amundsen, believing (erroneously) that the barrier was not free-floating ice but safely over land, set up camp there in 1911. His success, the aging explorer had argued to Byrd shortly before his death, proved that it was solid, and a suitable spot for the American's proposed wintering-over camp. Its snow-covered surface was perfect for modern planes equipped with skis. Besides, at 80 degrees south, the inlet was a mere six hundred miles from the South Pole—the nearest a ship could approach and the easiest point of takeoff for a pilot aiming to fly over the pole.

Byrd planned to establish bases at hundred-mile intervals all the way to the pole, manned by the bravest men in layers of long underwear, wool sweaters, bearskin trousers, reindeer-skin coats, and sealskin gloves. Only the best of his men—those that had proved their mettle—would winter over, spending six months in total darkness before Byrd and his new chief pilot, Bernt Balchen, could make their South Pole flight when the sun returned. One of Byrd's strengths was his vigilance for safety, but, even so, there were real and exciting dangers ahead. Beat reporters said the coldest temperature recorded in Antarctica was minus 74.4 degrees, with the strongest winds on Earth. The newsies knew their audience: What young man didn't dream of battling windstorms and rolling waves?

Alas, expeditions gobbled money before they even entered water, and despite Byrd's best efforts, funds were still short—though in nine months, he'd raised $900,000 (in the dollars of the day). His two principal backers were John D. Rockefeller Jr. and Edsel Ford, the thirty-five-year-old son of Henry Ford, who had succeeded his father as president of the Ford Motor Company in 1919. But while checks from private donors constituted the bulk of his cash, media rights also sold for a pretty penny: the *New York Times* paid $150,000 to be the official newspaper of the expedition, a deal that included assigning Russell Owen on board the flagship to dispatch stories by wireless. Byrd also secured $50,000 from his friend George Putnam for an autobiographical account of his journey, financing from the National Geographic Society for magazine rights, and a handsome sum from Paramount Pictures for the honor of sending a two-man crew with the ships to shoot a documentary at sea and on the ice— even if Paramount had to pay salaries for a two-year job.

Many expenses were avoided through in-kind donations of close to $600,000 in goods, an unimaginable sum possible only because Byrd traded favors shamelessly—as much a wheeler-dealer as he was a voyager. (He was, to be fair, only following the Antarctic business model: that fine British gentleman Robert Falcon Scott had financed his famous 1911 journey by chasing sponsorship, including one ton of donated Colman's mustard.) Cargo would soon include Kolster-Brandes radios "drawn from the crucible of science"; Hamilton stopwatches for officers ("The one place you would think time would be unimportant would be at the South Pole"); Leica and Graflex cameras for the pilots and media types; and Waterman pens engraved with the words *New York.* There would be Underwood typewriters, Longines chronometers, Kitchen Kook stoves, Veedol motor oil, National Ammonia brand ammonia, Flit brand insect repellent, and axes and hammers from Fayette R. Plumb. Sponsors donated refrigerators, binoculars, microscopes, United Fruit bananas, and caseloads of Chesterfield cigarettes. Beech-Nut committed to peanut butter, jams, and jellies; Swift was good for calf's liver, oxtail, pork loins, pigs' feet, "frankfurts," turkeys, and fowl. Brookfield Dairy supplied the "official" butter. Armour took out smoked-meat ads in which it noted that Byrd had already taken the company's ham and bacon to the North Pole. And in addition to shelled Diamond brand walnuts, the Byrd South Pole expedition would take along a hundred-pound gunny sack of Diamond's unshelled nuts, 3,180 calories per pound.

Sweets were of special interest to the boys and girls following along, and Necco anticipated great press for the rolls of candy wafers it was sending south. Byrd received a last-minute letter from William Wrigley Jr. of Chicago, who had instructed his factory in Dunedin, New Zealand, to send five hundred pounds of chewing gum to Antarctica to avoid having it pass through the tropics. The members of the expedition would be familiar with peppermint, Wrigley wrote, but they would also discover an exotic flavor called spearmint already on market in New Zealand—an offering Wrigley hoped the expedition would publicize, as the product was launching shortly in American stores.

With all these favors to beg and sponsors to thank, Byrd was exhausted before even leaving New York; he had to prioritize his speaking engagements, or he would never get to bed. No more formal dinners like that with the National Association of the Fur Industry, broadcast live on radio, at which he was presented with sixty muskrat fur caps, sixty Siberian dog fur gloves, and thirty pieces of wolverine so their winter parkas could be fitted with wolverine strips to cover the chin and mouth, as it was the only known fur on which the moisture of human breath would not freeze.

For the most part, journalists remained respectful of the hero-turned-promoter. The only ones daring enough to poke occasional fun at the never-ending plugs were those roundtable wits at the *New Yorker*, a magazine then only three years old but already wielding considerable literary influence. Said one Talk of the Town piece, with studied ennui:

"There is one item in the published expense account which tends to shed light on what the explorers are going to be doing way down there at the pole; that is the item Kardex and office supplies, $2,500. Apparently they'll be busy every minute with bookkeeping and general office management. Every night someone is in for a big job of filing—we can see that." (Although the piece was anonymous, an in-person check at the *New Yorker* offices revealed it was written by underappreciated wit E. B. White.)

By late summer, his bank accounts now fattened enough to at last set sail, Byrd toned down his rhetoric and focused on selling the expedition's respectable scientific goals. Officially his main purpose was to aerially map vast geography the world had never known and to highlight how aviation could benefit exploration.

"The expedition will be in many respects one of the most novel expeditions which ever moved its way into the regions of ice," Byrd said in late August, standing a little taller, more hero-like, in the

Biltmore conference room; he was now giving an official update once a week. He envisioned great new advances in geography via aerial photography. They would search for new animals and even dinosaur fossils. His engineers would try out the latest developments in shortwave radio, allowing the world to listen in on his exploits as they happened in Morse code (voice transmission from Antarctica then being impractical if not impossible). Still, a few naysayers whispered that the main business of the two-year expedition was immortalizing Byrd himself.

Yes, for good measure, as everyone knew, he was going to be the first to fly over the South Pole. Norway had gotten there first on foot, but flight was the prize left for America. It was something everyone could get behind, from the youngest citizen to the oldest. (Privately, Byrd felt it would broaden his name recognition in other countries, too. His PR men had wisely cautioned him that without the Inuit men and women populating the colony—Nukaping had been uninvited long before, as the idea of a breeding colony of Inuits was in reality a logistical nightmare—he needed a new gimmick.)

As the general excitement built in the days leading up to the *City of New York*'s launch, even Billy's mother clipped the daily newspaper updates, though Francesca shared her husband's view that applying to join was a pipe dream: with the sensational news from Cooper Union, he should just enjoy the unfolding Byrd story in the papers.

Improbably, it was Billy's no-nonsense father—not his grandmother with the crystal ball—who one day in mid-August let slip a fateful fact: Rudy had read that Malcolm Hanson, the chief radio operator on the upcoming Antarctica journey, had been a stowaway on Byrd's 1926 Arctic expedition. A stowaway! Could such a thing be possible?

And thus Billy Gawronski hatched an outlandish plan to stow away on the first great American voyage of the twentieth century.

THREE

THE CITY OF NEW YORK

As he took his first strokes through the murky, reeking Hudson River, Billy feared the whipping winds. He kept count—one, two, three, four, five; six, seven, eight, nine, ten—feeling a growing ease in the choppy water, even if he wasn't going as fast as he thought. "Keep going," he told himself; it was less than a mile to the ship. So long ago, on outdoor swims with the Polish Falcons, he had mastered the right way to breathe. Later, a streetwise immigrant's kid, he'd jumped off the East River pier at a roped-off swimming area called Central Lanes, where even as a nine-year-old, he faced a harsher current than here. Billy was a veteran of hundreds of river swims.

As he told it later, the only thing on his mind was his one shot to get before Commander Byrd and appeal to his mercy. Byrd liked stowaways. All the seventeen-year-old could do was aim for the flag-ship and hope for the best.

As he approached the *City of New York*, there was enough light to spot a hawser (a thick tow rope) hanging down to the brackish water. Despite numb fatigue, Billy found the strength to pull himself up and then keep his footing on the slippery deck that smelled of salt and masculine adventure. Covered in river scum, hair hanging down his forehead like oily kelp, he found his way to the hold, clamber-ing on hands and knees, inching crabwise over rough-hewn wooden boards, and picking his way past intriguing crates of explorer sup-plies to find the out-of-view spot he'd settled on during his recon-naissance mission nine days before.

Billy removed his squelchy wet graduation suit, rolled the jacket and pants out of view, and stripped to his underwear. (One contra-dictory account claimed that he hid nude.) Secreted in the pitch-black of the smaller of the two forecastles he'd selected when the ship was open to visitors, Billy retold himself there had to be a job on the ship for a determined kid like him with water-clogged ears. Did he think of his mother, so fiercely protective of her only child; a woman who would never have thought him capable of betraying her this way? How long could he hold out without food or water? When should he emerge? There was no official rulebook for stowaways.

He had read about the hoopla planned for the send-off in the morning: the brass bands and relatives and bigwigs invited on deck to say good-bye before the *New York* loosened her moorings and the city's official welcoming tugboat brought well-wishers back to shore. Rumor had it that Amelia Earhart, the new Queen of the Air, would loop-de-loop over the Hudson, the grand finale to send the ship on its way. Earhart was a great friend of Commander Byrd, and, unbeknownst to the public, the new mistress of his very mar-ried publisher. She had promoted the expedition as a personal favor, endorsing Lucky Strike cigarettes ("Lucky Strikes were the cigarettes she carried on the *Friendship* when she crossed the Atlantic. For a slender figure, Reach for a Lucky instead of a sweet") and publicly handing over her $1,500 earnings to fund the Antarctic trip.

Finally, snatches of sleep until—something creaked. A rat? Scary shadows flickered across the walls. What happened next felt like a hallucination: just a few feet away from him on the dark second forecastle deck, Billy could just see a kid around his age, equally shocked to have company. The puny boy whispered his name: Jack.

Jack was a happy-go-lucky sixteen-year-old Jewish kid who had dropped out of school. Before this caper, Manhattan was the farthest he'd ever traveled from the Brownsville section of Brooklyn, where he'd been born. Jack told his unexpected competitor that he'd arrived at the *City of New York* at seven o'clock in the morning, an hour before.

Well, determined Billy, then he was here first, hours ago. This was his spot.

Jack tried to discourage Billy, insisting that it wouldn't pay for him to make this two-year trip without any of the thought he himself had put in. Why, Jack had brought a suitcase stuffed with warm clothes for once they neared Antarctica. He'd come aboard with extra clean underwear and a $100 bill pinned inside a coat pocket. Billy was practically naked. Negative 74.4 degrees? He'd freeze!

Billy was no dupe. "Is that so?" he shot back. If this was going to be such a rotten trip, why didn't Jack get off the boat?

The boys argued for nearly an hour, cramped in their almost-adjacent shelves on the lower hidden forecastle, first in whispers, and then louder and louder. But then, to their joint amazement, yet another voice piped up: "Keep quiet! They'll find all of us!"

Could there really be a *third* stowaway? Yes, the voice told them, for over two days! It was a deeper voice, manlier, belonging to one

Bob Lanier, a black youth of twenty. Even knowing where to look, Billy and Jack could see only his feet.

Well, Jack said, that still left him the "sensible" one who had thought this through. Who goes the cracked step of swimming in the Hudson? Nuts! He'd taken a ferry and entered from the Hoboken pier when the crew wasn't looking, without getting wet or tired out.

Bob said he had hired a rowboat to get to the ship, remaining as dry as Jack. Then he stopped talking, even when Billy and Jack called out to him. He let the younger daredevils bicker over who had the right to be with Byrd.

As the sun broke from behind clouds above deck, thousands of wistful Byrd fans jammed the pier. Nineteen Eagle Scouts were thickly clustered where the expedition publicists had prearranged for them to congratulate the cherry-picked Paul Siple, who, in full view of the cameras, calmly said good-bye to his tearful parents and his twenty-five-year-old sister, Carolyn, and admitted to curious reporters that, no, he didn't have a girl. One reporter later described Siple as "[t]he fully-accepted Peter Pan, standing on deck as calm as Capablanca." (Cuban-born José Raúl Capablanca was world chess champion from 1921 to 1927.)

Nearly six foot four and weighing more than two hundred pounds, Siple was hardly a boy in the same way that Billy or Jack was, and his Boy Scouts uniform bulged with telltale manly muscles. But the media kept up the charade, even though the nineteen-year-old had already completed his first year at Allegheny College in Meadville, Pennsylvania, his double majors biology and geology. (Byrd had shrewdly set an age of seventeen to twenty for his scouting recruitment.)

Below deck, the boys agreed, finally, on something: Siple had to be a ringer! He was a member of the Alpha Chi Rho fraternity. He was not a boy like them.

Up above the boys' heads, Commander Byrd had joined the flagship crew for a minitrip around the Statue of Liberty before his scheduled return to shore. Dressed in khaki trousers and shirt, and topped with a little khaki sunhat appropriate for the wilds of a jungle, Byrd was the very embodiment of what Americans thought an explorer should be.

As commotion increased above, adrenaline spiked below in the hold. The trio was terrified of being discovered before the ship left port. If only they could hear more than muffled voices.

Journalists fired off last questions, with Byrd pooh-poohing rumors that the two thousand gallons of booze, four hundred gallons of rum, one hundred gallons of port wine, one hundred gallons of sherry, one hundred quarts of champagne, and additional rye and burgundy on board were anything but medicinal. What an undignified question! "Just when we are starting," he told the goading reporter who dared to raise that issue now, "I can hardly afford to discuss things that are not so. I have issued the order that there is to be no intoxicating liquor aboard except for medicinal purposes, and that this alcohol is to be kept under lock and key by the medical officer of the expedition."

(The explorers of what's been called the heroic age did not have to suffer the indignity of American prudency: Ernest Shackleton wisely brought along plenty of hard liquor to cheer his men. In 2006 several unopened cases of the malt whisky his boozy crew imbibed in 1909 were found beneath the floorboards of their expedition hut in Antarctica's Cape Royds. The whisky was smartly cloned by the original distiller, Mackinlay's, for sale in the twenty-first century as Mackinlay's Shackleton Rare Old Highland Malt.)

The *City of New York* left Hoboken's Pier 1 with two hundred tons of material aboard and thirty-three people (not including three thrill-thirsty stowaways) shortly before one o'clock. Barges had been set up under spitting skies for hundreds of cheering spectators, and there was a band aboard New York City's official municipal welcoming tug, the *Macom* (its name an abbreviation of "Mayor's Committee"), an iconic boat built in 1894 and still in regular use for greeting visiting dignitaries, from foreign leaders to triumphant sports stars. The band's playlist included "The Star-Spangled Banner," "Auld Lang Syne," "Till We Meet Again," "While," and "Laugh! Clown! Laugh!"

Fireworks thrilled.

After a final speech, a Junkers monoplane manned by the expedition's much-lauded pilots dipped and capered across the voyaging ship's bows, and banked at vertiginous angles over her stem, the most forward part of a ship's bow. (Although some 1928 reporters thought aviatrix sensation Amelia Earhart was also circling overhead in tribute, others got it right: she had merely come aboard for the send-off.) Ships docked at piers and on the river whistled goodbye. Harold Cunningham, the captain of the largest working American ship, the *Leviathan*, swung his gargantuan liner to pay respect before heading to Rio de Janeiro. Well-heeled passengers in nautical sweaters and vested suits came to the rails, and—seeing the gold-and-blue banner for the "Byrd Antarctica Expedition" on the ship passing by—waved wildly. Next to the *Leviathan*, the forty-three-year-old square-rigger looked like a bathtub toy.

Up on deck of the *New York* stood the assigned *Times* reporter, Russell Owen, already a well-respected veteran of exploration coverage but not yet nearly the household name he would become by expedition's end. He'd later describe leaning against the railing and taking his first notes as an unofficial crew member while each swash of wave hit. Owen's dozens of articles over the next two years would earn him a Pulitzer Prize.

Just before the trip, Curtis D. Wilbur, the US secretary of the navy, had authorized a promotion as a favor for Byrd's PR team. Now, for the first time, Captain Frederick Melville wore a lieutenant commander of the Naval Reserves uniform. Amazed by the fuss, Melville gave an exclusive to *Boston Evening Transcript* reporter W. A. MacDonald, who, even before Russell Owen, had broken the story that Boston-based Byrd would head to the South Pole. MacDonald also received the go-ahead to stay on board as far as the lightship *Ambrose*—a floating lighthouse—at the nearby convergence of New York and New Jersey shipping lanes. "This is what I have always been used to, the sea," Herman Melville's second cousin said. "I have never had notoriety before. I like this. I am happy now."

Still down below and having missed all the revelries—and panicking a few times at the sound of nearby footsteps—the three hidden youths felt real motion now. Their bona fide adventure began as the *City of New York* slowly navigated the tricky waters of New York Harbor, heading toward the Atlantic Ocean and a quick first stop in Virginia to top up her coal briquettes before sailing for the Panama Canal.

Shirtless men in overalls scampered on deck, working to square the yards (adjust the sails) before hitting the Atlantic. Below deck a radio was turned on. Love songs were popular then as always—tunes such as Marion Harris's bluesy "The Man I Love," and "I Wanna Be Loved by You," sung in a high soprano by Helen Kane, the woman whose voice and appearance inspired the animated Betty Boop.

Did the boys discuss a plan to emerge? Did they even have one? Byrd would disembark soon, yes—but even if they were found before he left after sailing a few miles with reporters for show, they'd have plenty of opportunity to meet their hero in Dunedin, after all, in two months' time.

The *City of New York* passed the forty-two-year-old Statue of Liberty, a landmark willed into being by a man after Billy's own heart: tenacious French sculptor Frédéric Auguste Bartholdi, who had been rejected by the brass over at the Suez Canal, where he originally envisioned the mammoth monument to stand. Following that, he refocused on placing the statue in Central Park, but those plans fell apart, too. Near the Narrows, the ship passed Brooklyn's historic Fort Hamilton, where soldiers of the newly formed United States of America fired at British troopships on July, 4, 1776, the day the Declaration of Independence was signed into law. Next, the *New York* reached the tidal strait separating Staten Island and Brooklyn (now spanned by the vast Verrazano-Narrows Bridge, for many years the longest suspension bridge in the world). Byrd was pleased: his flagship had made it without a hitch almost to Ambrose Channel, where the last reporters would depart by pilot boat back to New Jersey. Mrs. Byrd and their son, Dickie (and assorted dignitaries), had just been taken away by tugboat; the *City of New York* had been officially released.

Nerves frayed, sloppy with exhaustion, Billy and Jack were at it again, not even in hiding anymore. Why wouldn't a young fellow like Billy be thinking of getting a start in the world instead of traveling around? He'd have to work awfully hard if they caught him, and he wouldn't be paid for it.

Footsteps! Someone above had heard Jack and Billy arguing: that someone being sharp-eyed Sverre Strom, the six-foot-two, two-hundred-pound Norwegian second mate and ice pilot—one of the very few foreigners invited to join the Americans. Everyone wanted Norwegians. Strom had been hired as a veteran of the *Samson* when it sailed under his country's flag. He had ten years' experience at sea, and, unlike most of the newbie volunteer passengers, he knew how things were supposed to run.

Hearing Strom's voice, Billy dashed to the bunker in a desperate attempt to hide again. But no luck. He was caught, pinned down by Strom's strong tattooed arms until backup could come.

Delaying his own inevitable fate, the yet-undetected Jack ducked down until the opportune moment when he could tear for the stern, breathing hard as he entered and latched the washroom behind him.

"I'm sure there were two boys, not just one," Strom told Captain Melville, who came down to see what the ruckus was. But Billy wasn't talking.

Melville was a stern man, and he knew what to do with a truant ferreted out from his hidey-hole—even this unimposing kid shivering and dizzy and stripped to his underwear. But Byrd wanted to speak to the boy. The ship was stopped not far from the Statue of Liberty, and Billy, not at all as he had envisioned it, was brought above deck to come face-to-face with the commander. With the strong scent of the sea scud still upon him, Billy trembled.

Byrd greeted him in a sharp tenor voice and the distinct twang of a well-bred Shenandoah Valley Virginian. He asked for the boy's clothes to be brought on deck so that the near-naked kid could have some dignity. "What's your name, young man?" Byrd probed gently, but Billy was too ashamed to speak. He was so upset that he would not tell who he was even when Byrd said he liked his spirit. By all accounts, Byrd was a gentle interrogator. He said he understood the tearful kid was an adventurer like him and told him not to be scared. They only needed his name so they could contact his parents, who must be worried. But Billy sobbed. Humiliated, seething, he put on his wet, crumpled suit and was told to sit until the *Macom* tug could be recalled to take him away.

At Sandy Hook, New Jersey, a nose past New York City, the miserable truant was placed in the hands of a customs inspector and sent back toward Hoboken, an unusual catch plucked from the sea. Far away on the horizon, back in the direction from which he came, sparkled the lights of the Coney Island amusement park and the Far Rockaway beaches where Billy had joined the Polish Falcons on swims. Was a lifetime spent practicing for this moment supposed to have better prepared him than this?

STOWAWAY FOUND IN HOLD!

Deep in the archives of the New York Public Library, filed under *New York Times* accounting, is the receipt for the $5 that Byrd's secretary-turned-yeoman, Charley Lofgren, received for letting a *Times* reporter know he had a good story for him in this kid. The *Boston Evening Transcript* reporter on board might have mentioned an angry stowaway, but Lofgren had a photo for the *Times* of him scowling, and more details.

The following day, August 26, the editors of the *New York Times* splashed Billy's face on the front cover: the poor mite with rumpled dreams and hair, photographed shortly after his discovery. Charitably, someone had lent him a tie to wear with his wet, bedraggled high school graduation suit. Under the sensational headline, a taunting caption: "Boy so angry at being found that he refused to give his name."

The *New York Daily News* quipped, "Of course there had to be a stowaway. He was a small boy, who wept with disappointment, and refused to give his name." If Billy sought significance, the pitiful photo, though it attracted front-page coverage, made him seem very insignificant indeed.

A different, glorious photo ran side by side with Billy's on the front page of the *New York Times*, this one of Paul Siple, the clean-cut Eagle Scout from the Pennsylvania boonies, photographed kissing his mother. It was captioned "The Luckiest Boy of All."

But what of the other stowaways?

It was the good old chief engineer, Thomas "Mac" Mulroy, a Scottish fellow who had been the ground officer for Byrd's transatlantic flight in 1927, who, as the radio blared from the poop deck, caught "the Jewish stowaway" in the locked washroom after noticing a rag in the ventilator. The ruddy-faced Mulroy tried the door and heard, as the *Brooklyn Daily Eagle* put it, "the stealthy movement of feet."

"Got him!" he yelled; the scared kid was hiding between the wall and the bathtub.

Bony, curly haired Jack lied to Mulroy that his name was Jack Solomon and he lived in Manhattan, even coming up with a fake address of 98 East Seventh Street.

Mulroy brought the second malingerer to Commander Byrd, who laughed loudly and said, "Hello, son!" He introduced him to Mrs. Byrd, who had rejoined her husband on board when the *Macom* returned to take away Billy, as "our latest stowaway!"

Jack Solomon was actually Jack Solowitz of 336 Dumont Avenue in Brownsville, Brooklyn, the second-oldest of eleven siblings, who hadn't learned English until the first grade. He'd been a runner delivering market orders to a broker's floor trader on Wall Street but had been unemployed for several months, making money off of craps games, whenever he heard the familiar tinkle of dice. (He would later tell his sons that by sixteen, he had saved a nest egg of $1,000 in stocks, buying on margin. Craps was a game of skill, not chance, he said. If you were good at math, you could make money. You could make money with loaded dice, too.)

Byrd told Jack that he was "undersized" to be on the crew even as a lowly seaman. But he assured the kid, in words similar to those he said to Billy, "You've got good spirit." In a burst of altruism, Byrd asked an officer to lend him $10 so that he might offer it to the young man. This was not the climactic moment Jack had envisioned, either, and he refused to take it. But he did accept Byrd's calling card with a scribbled note that he'd met the boy and liked him. Maybe that would help him get a job—perhaps on the supply ship that would join the expedition later, if he formally applied. Byrd was startled to hear the kid ask for his valise, packed with enough clothes to take him around the globe.

Off the northeastern shore of Staten Island, with the flagship still within New York City's boundaries, Jack was removed to a tug called the *Scout* and, like Billy, sent back to Hoboken.

Just as the youngest Polish Catholics would soon have an anti-hero in Billy Gawronski, the Jews had their own stowaway to cheer for after Jack's story was picked up in Yiddish and English in the burgeoning Jewish press, and then in the national press.

JEWISH BOY TRIES TO GO WITH BYRD IN NEW YORK!

Macy's would even run an underwear ad for Kait Union Suits (selling for $1.88), inspired by Jack's foresight.

ANTARCTIC STOWAWAY TOOK HIS "HEAVIES" ALONG

Practical stowaway found clutching his "winter undies" and a coat under the forecastle deck. But alas, for romance, adventure and travel, the ambitious stowaway was discovered. Even if your boy isn't an antarctic stowaway, stow away some winter "Heavies" for him. Have him ready for the South Pole-ish weather that is sure to come!

Jack told one newspaper that he had been among the two thousand tourists inspecting the *City of New York* back on August 15. Had he crossed paths with Billy that day? (The sixteen-year-old continued his shenanigans back on land: two months later, he tried another escape out of Brooklyn as an aerial stowaway on the *Graf Zeppelin*,

sister airship to the *Hindenburg*. He was found in the engine na-
celle, a stand-alone compartment on the dirigible. Kicked off, he then
boarded the gondola, the lower part of the great ship, only to be
caught again.)

Jack and Billy were together in detention in Hoboken as they
awaited their parents. Did they speak? If they wondered whether
the black stowaway had been found, they did not rat him out. What
kind of fink would do that?

Sverre Strom, the brawny second mate, finally uncovered the
third stowaway less than an hour later. Bob Lanier was found during a routine check by flashlight in the head of the lower forecastle,
wedged between a spare propeller blade and the side of the ship. The
timing! Byrd was just about to leave the ship. Upon being discovered, Bob staggered to his feet and said, "I'm all right. Just a little
stiff." He clutched a silver pencil and the notebook he meant to write
his memoirs in; on his back, he had an old army knapsack. Bob admitted to Strom that he'd been in hiding without food or water for
three days—even during cyanide gas fumigation to clear pests off the
ship—and that he had been secreted for four days before that on the
beams beneath the pier, waiting for the opportune moment to climb
onto the ship. He'd planned to come out only when it was too far
for him to be sent home.

Lanier's blackness was bothering to a bigoted country. Newspaper reports of his discovery smack of prevailing racism in the
early twentieth century, starting with this alternate version of events
from an uncredited *Times* reporter, which was likely written by the
esteemed Russell Owen: "The odor of watermelon wafted down
from the ship's galley . . . proved too much for him on the third day,
and he crawled out, went to the captain and begged to be forgiven
and taken along."

Coverage was even crueler in small-town America, where

headlines out of New York were rewritten to "Watermelon Trips Byrd Ship Stowaway" and "Melon Lures Hiding Negro."

In Paul Siple's journal, which he kept dutifully to help his ghost-writer with his book promised to George Putnam, he admitted being the one to feed Lanier the watermelon. On the same page, he jotted down a note revealing his own provincial upbringing: "He sure showed his nationality." Fifty-nine merit badges, but none for lack of prejudice.

Bob Lanier was the last truant brought before the commander, who marveled at the scourge of stowaways of every ethnicity. A Pole and a Jew and a black man stowed away . . . It was the start of a bad joke. Bob told Byrd he was a twenty-year-old orphan who lived with his sister, a Mrs. Helen Gant of 29 Orient Avenue, Jersey City, and was employed as a messenger in a Jersey City factory. He brazenly claimed to have walked across America in 1925. In stowing away, he had been inspired by the first black man to reach the North Pole, Matthew Henson, who'd sledged over snow with Admiral Robert Peary and his husky dogs in 1909.

"I have read all about your Boy Scout Paul Siple," Bob said, "and I too had also been a Boy Scout since I was eleven, but I know I would have barely had a chance as a colored kid unless I could show you how exceptional I was."

"By Jove, I admire that Negro!" Byrd said in front of W. A. MacDonald, the newsie from Boston. "What am I going to do with a man like that?"

Luckily for Bob, Byrd had just learned that the *City of New York* was one man short. The young bride of one the crew members had her husband kidnapped that morning so he couldn't join the expedition.

A few minutes later, the new dishwasher on the *New York* was determined: Robert "Bob" Lanier.

His selection irked many Americans who could not understand

why he would have been given the job over a white man. Up popped Bob Lanier's supposed factory bosses, described by wire services as "welfare workers and prominent Negroes," who claimed he was once arrested for disorderly conduct. Even so, he was on his way to Antarctica—for now.

Black Americans who followed the Byrd stowaway story were horrified by what they were reading in much of the press. Appreciating Robert White Lanier's historical significance, a particularly exulting editorial was published in the *Pittsburgh Courier*, the largest black paper in circulation. Two pages long, it offered a timeline of the greatest accomplishments by black men and women in American history, from a black man piloting one of Christopher Columbus's ships, to blacks in Jamestown, Virginia—the first permanent English settlement in America—in the sixteen hundreds, to Matthew Henson, among the first to reach the geographic North Pole, and ending with pride: "The promoter of the first trip to the moon had better examine the rocket carefully if they would make sure that no adventurous Negro is aboard."

The three stowaways quickly became part of the nation's psyche, their adventures ripe for parody. A bogus stowaway named "J. Hermann Seidlitz" was birthed by nationally syndicated *New York Evening World* humorist Neal O'Hara: "yet another" Byrd scalawag discovered between a crate of playing cards and a hogshead of phonograph needles. The fake stowaway's semiregular reports were dispatched for the next two years through O'Hara's Telling the World column, sent in by dogsled and homing pigeon. Millions chuckled reading Seidlitz's "true accounts." That a Jew, a Pole, and a black man were hiding in the forecastle was not just the beginning of a joke; their stories struck a chord with readers because they represented a microcosm of American barriers and dreams.

Indeed, so many across the country delighted in this vicarious chance to stow away that the *Brooklyn Daily Eagle* couldn't help but muse, "We only wonder why there were but three stowaways on Commander Byrd's bark, the *City of New York?*"

Back in Bayside, Rudy and Francesca were beside themselves, with no note or word from their son. Did he have any idea what turmoil he had caused? Unbeknownst to Billy, as he hid on the shores of New Jersey the previous evening, there had been a rush-hour catastrophe: a ten-car derailment beneath Times Square of an Interborough Rapid Transit (IRT) subway train carrying 1,800 commuters. The breaking news of the second-worst train wreck in New York City history (then and now) led the radio broadcasts and the headlines of the evening papers. Dozens were reported killed. With Billy still gone the following morning, Rudy and Francesca had feared the worst.

Their son was alive but publicly humiliated, his disheveled picture on the front page of the papers. What was to become of his now-muddled career path?

After an unpleasant car ride back home with his father from Hoboken detention to Bayside, he did not get any smiles from his parents. What kind of hero breaks the law? Any moral arguments about how he had failed them did not sink in. Upstairs with his bedroom locked, Billy was discouraged but "not licked."

FOUR

THE TRIUMPH OF THE CENTURY

A dogged *New York Times* reporter found out Billy's name, give or take a few letters, and the portrait of an unidentified disheveled raga-muffin that previously graced the first page ran a second time, this time on the front of its photogravure magazine section, called *New York Times Mid-Week Pictorial*. The "paper of record" misspelled his last name as Gravenski. Even so, Billy's ascent as a boy hero among New York youth had begun immediately after he first made news.

The amusing multiple-stowaway story made an even bigger splash in nationally circulated *Time* magazine, but even there, jour-nalists printed the name Gravenski. (One reporter quipped that the considerable store of booze could account for the fact that they found "another stowaway or two on the flagship every time they looked it over.")

The *Brooklyn Daily Eagle* saw a great local story to expand; many of its expedition articles now focused on Billy, who was, it announced in a scoop, "Doomed to Study Interior Decoration." After divulging that he was to start Cooper Union in mid-September, the (finally) correctly identified William Gawronski, choked with tears, told the *Eagle*'s reporter: "I thought [Byrd] might let me go when he realized I, too, was willing to dare anything or put up with any hardship in order to be with him." He probably cried even more when news broke that one of the other stowaways was on his way to the Panama Canal.

Rudy calmed Francesca as best as he could when their boy's face was on the front page of the *New York Times* not once but twice. But now the distressing episode was behind them, wasn't it, except for a little residual shame?

As night dropped on September 15, Billy jumped out of his second-floor window and onto the garden, a fall softened by potatoes and cabbage plants and proudly photographed sunflowers. You would think that the boy had learned from his previous stowaway attempt to bring more food or a change of dry clothes. Not the case.

An overnight subway crossing into Brooklyn took him to the Tebo Yacht Basin in Gowanus. He made for the location he'd written down in his notes: Third Avenue and Twenty-Third Street.

In 1928 William Todd's Tebo Yacht Basin was a resting spot—*the* spot—for the yachts of the Atlantic seaboard's most aristocratic and prosperous residents. The swanky yard berthed more than fifty staggering prizes of the filthy rich. Railroad executive Cornelius Vanderbilt kept his yacht *O-We-Ra* here; John Vanneck, his *Amphitrite*. Here was also where to find *Warrior*, the largest private yacht afloat, owned by the wealthiest man in America, public utilities baron Harrison Williams; yeast king (and former mayor of

Cincinnati) Julian Fleischman's $625,000 twin-screw diesel yacht, the *Carmago*; General Motors president Alfred P. Sloan's *Rene*; shoe scion H. W. Hanan's *Dauntless*; and J. P. Morgan's *Corsair III*. The Tebo Yacht Basin's clubroom served fish chowder luncheons to millionaires in leather-backed mission chairs.

Todd, a great friend of Byrd's, lavished attention on his superconnected pal with more contacts than dollars. He had provided major funding for Byrd's 1926 flight over the North Pole, and helped the commander locate and refit two of the four Antarctic expedition ships for $285,900, done at cost. Todd loved puffy articles about him as much as the next man, and press would help extract cash from the millionaires he actively pursued as new clients; helping out a famous friend might prove cheaper than the advertisements he placed in up-market magazines. Throughout that summer, Byrd mentioned Todd's generous support frequently.

Two weeks after the *City of New York* set sail, the *Chelsea*, the supply ship of the expedition, was still docked at the Tebo workyard and not scheduled to depart until the middle of September. Smith's Dock Company in England had built the refurbished 170-foot, 800-ton iron freighter for the British Royal Navy at the tail end of the Great War. First christened patrol gunboat HMS *Kilmarnock*, her name was changed to the *Chelsea* during her post–Royal Navy rum-running days.

Not long before she was scheduled to depart, Byrd announced via a press release that he was renaming this auxiliary ship, too, after his mother, Eleanor Bolling. But the name painted on the transom was *Eleanor Boling*, with one *l*—the painter's mistake. As distressing as this was (the name was his mother's, after all), Byrd felt a redo would be too expensive and a silly use of precious funds. Reporters and PR staff were simply instructed to always spell the name with two *l*s.

As Billy eyed the ship in dock days after his humiliation on board the *New York*, he realized here was another way to get to Antarctica. The old, rusty-sided cargo ship would likely be less guarded than the flagship had been.

As September dragged on, Billy, back in Bayside, stiffened his resolve. No one would think he'd try again! On September 15, once more he swam out during the night to board a vessel bound for Antarctica.

Since his visit two weeks prior, Billy had studied his news clippings and knew that the *Bolling* was captained by thirty-six-year-old Gustav L. Brown, who'd been promoted weeks earlier from first mate of the *New York* when Byrd added the fourth ship to his fleet. Billy liked what he read. According to those who sailed under Brown's command, this tall and slender veteran of the Great War was above all genteel, and far less crotchety than the *New York*'s Captain Melville. Captain Brown's education went only as far as high school, and while he wasn't against college, he admired honest, down-to-earth workers. Like his colleague Captain Melville, Brown had begun a seafaring life at fourteen. He seemed just the sort of man to take a liking to a teenage stowaway with big dreams.

Alas, the crew of the second ship headed to Antarctica now knew to look for stowaways. In a less dramatic repeat of what had happened in Hoboken, an *Eleanor Bolling* seaman ousted Billy in the earliest hours of the morning. The kid had (unimaginatively) hidden for a second time in a locker under the lower forecastle filled with mops and bolts and plumbing supplies. The sailor brought him to Captain Brown, who was well named, as he was a man with a mass of brown hair and warm brown eyes. The kind captain smiled at Billy and praised the cheeky boy's gumption—his Swedish accent still heavy even though he'd made Philadelphia his home since 1920—yet Billy was escorted off to the dock and told to scram.

A few hours later, still under the cover of night, Billy stole back on board and was routed out a third time, again from the "paint locker."

A third time? The *Bolling*'s third in command, Lieutenant Harry Adams, took notes on the gutsy kid who *had* to be good material for the lucrative book he secretly hoped to pen. Most of the major players would score book deals after the expedition; the public was eager for adventure, or at least so publishers thought. The catch was that any deal had to be approved by Byrd: to expose any discord was to risk powerful support. Adams's book, *Beyond the Barrier with Byrd: An Authentic Story of the Byrd Antarctic Exploring Expedition*, was among the best: more character study than thriller, his grand sense of humor evident in his selection of anecdotes that the others deemed too lightweight to include.

Billy was not the only stowaway that September day. Also aboard was a girl Adams called Sunshine, the "darling of the expedition," a flirt who offered to anyone who asked that she wanted to be the first lady in Antarctica. (In the restless era between world wars, when movies gave everyone big dreams, even girl stowaways were not uncommon.) Brown told a reporter that Sunshine had less noble aspirations, and soon she, too, was removed from the *Bolling*, but not before she gave each crew member a theatrical kiss.

As the early sun rose, Captain Brown called Billy over to him from the yacht yard's holding area where he had been asked to wait with the giggling Sunshine until his father arrived. The captain admired Billy's gumption, but it was time for the seventeen-year-old to go now and not waste any more of anyone's time.

As Lieutenant Adams recorded later, "Perhaps this matter of

getting rid of Bill was entered up in the *Eleanor Bolling* log as the first scientific achievement of the Byrd Antarctic expedition."

Poor Captain Brown had quite the day. Soon after Billy and Sunshine were given the boot, another unwanted and unnamed guest, "a bewhiskered old fellow with Bible in hand," boarded the ship and prophesied doom. As if that would stop twenty men setting off for adventure.

On Monday, September 16, at exactly 6:13 a.m., after three whistle blasts, the *Bolling* shoved off for Norfolk, Virginia, with considerably less fanfare than her sister ship the *New York* had and no Commander Byrd present for the official send-off. Still, the *Bolling* had impressive crew aboard doing eyebrow-raising double duty. Both flying ace Captain Ashley "Ash" McKinley and John S. "Jack" O'Brien, a shift engineer and inspector at New York City's Holland Tunnel, doubled as coal passers. Esteemed geologist and landlubber Laurence Gould, who had accompanied Gyp Putnam on his expedition to Baffin Island, found himself boatswain, the "bell-bottom" assigned to look over equipment. Dr. Haldor Barnes, a prominent Danish surgeon based in Detroit, who was to be the assistant medical officer once the expedition reached the ice, was presently a first-time quartermaster—tasked with rationing clothing and rooms—unless he had to stitch up someone. William Haines, a respected meteorologist, was for now an assistant steward.

A brave black-and-white kitten had ventured on board overnight: the sailors promptly named her Eleanor after their vessel, and the resident reporter wisely turned this feline stowaway into the supply ship's own mascot—a soulmate of sorts to Captain Brown's tomcat, Rudy, and the *New York*'s kittens, tiger-striped Mary and little grey Winnie Winkle. Readers loved cats.

Billy was in some ways fortunate to miss the first brief stretch of the *Bolling*'s adventure. Halfway to the Virginia Cape (where they would load up on coal), the crew suffered the indignity of being boarded by vigilante Coast Guard commanding warrant officer Carl Grenager, who pulled up on an armed revenue cutter with a team of United States Marshals, suspecting a boat with "Byrd Antarctic Expedition" painted boldly on her side of being a rumrunner. From the deck of his government boat, Officer Grenager (rather hilariously) called, "Heave to 'til I board you!" (The *New Yorker* shortly quipped: "To this zealous . . . officer goes this department's infrequent award of the nickel-plated dumbbell.")

The crew soon encountered real trouble on the upper Atlantic. The trawler endured terrible storms, capped by one with winds eighty nautical miles strong off the outer banks of Cape Hatteras, the easternmost point on the southern seaboard—a shock to all. (Cape Hatteras is farther south than Norfolk; in the poor weather, they had slightly overshot their destination.) Many of the boat's academics and volunteers, greenhorns at sea, were seasick. Worse still: the night before, due to high winds, Captain Brown had lost contact with Commander Byrd, who had been following his path by Morse code. Byrd was now justly petrified that a good portion of his crew had drowned. His expedition would be over, humiliatingly, and so close to home.

Close to noon on September 19, two days later than scheduled, the *Eleanor Bolling* limped in to Norfolk's Hampton Roads Naval Base—home during the Civil War to the Confederate States Army—where much to the relief of the waylaid crew on board, their beleaguered ship was tied up at the bustling modernized port's Pier 2.

That's when Billy popped into view on the dock. The crew members, drained from the tempest, faces spattered with grease, cheered out loud. The Bayside kid! Holy cow!

Billy had ridden home from the Tebo Yacht Basin in his father's

Model A two days before, getting the talking-to of a lifetime, when the twice-scandalized Francesca met the Model A. After hours of chiding, he was sent to his bedroom in disgrace. Only he didn't sleep: sometime in the middle of the night, he escaped again out an open window from the second floor, once more without a suitcase. Billy thumbed a ride south, telling each gullible automobilist that he was a last-minute employ on the expedition—a replacement scrub-deck-and-bottle-washer—but only if he could reach the ship in time. Each delighted driver drove as fast as he could get away with; one sympathetic man even took him directly to the dock. This time Billy waited for the ship in plain sight.

George Tennant, the chubby-cheeked and wry chief cook, was tickled by the city kid's pluck and summoned Billy for a private word. Tennant, toothless and nicknamed "Gummy," had lived since his youth on South Street in New York's charitable Seamen's Church Institute of New York, an organization affiliated with the Episcopal Church to seek dignity for sailors. Tennant's formal education had stopped after grammar school, and he valued the young Polish striver's industriousness. The privileged volunteers never needed to develop this trait—those fellows born under a lucky star, like the millionaire's kid coal passer, Joe de Ganahl, whose father owned sugar plantations in Mexico; or heavy-drinking twenty-six-year-old George "Mike" Thorne, a seaman over on the *New York*. He was the Yale-educated grandson of George Thorne Sr., one of the founders of Chicago department store Montgomery Ward, who had contributed significant money to Byrd's cause. De Ganahl, a graduate of Harvard and Yale Universities, spoke with a posh private school accent. He'd been handed the coveted *Times* assignment to fill in bits of information that reporter Russell Owen would miss; after all, Owen couldn't be in two places at once. And he was a Freemason, of course, like Commander Byrd: that was no secret.

No, Tennant grumbled, even though he was a Freemason himself, kids like that weren't the ones who deserved to be on board.

The red-bearded forty-six-year-old cook tentatively offered Billy a job as a mess boy; Commander Byrd, who would be down to see the ship off, would have final say. But he suggested the kid stay put and start washing dishes if he wanted things to work out officially.

Billy beamed and then Tennant did, too, revealing smile-crinkles around his eyes. He whispered that he had real ins with Byrd; he had been a cook on the commander's expedition to the North Pole.

Tennant reminded Billy of a once well-known story about how, just after the turn of the century, Byrd fought for his father's permission to travel to the Philippines to visit Judge Adam "Kit" Carson, a family friend and the twelve-year-old's godfather, who was presiding over a bit of Manila after the Philippine-American War of 1899 to 1902. The young Byrd wouldn't stop asking until his mother took his side; she knew Carson would never let her son get in true danger. But still, a preteen traveling with five hundred soldiers made the papers: Virginia's *Winchester Star* called the boy a "manly and handsome youth, plucky and aggressive and brave as a lion," and wrote that "Dick [was] the youngest person to take such a long journey alone." That was what had first put Byrd's name on the map: his tenacity. Tennant would remind his boss of this, and mention—no small thing to a man keen on camaraderie—that the crew of the *Bolling* loved Billy's spirit; that they'd clapped and hollered when they spied him on the dock.

When Captain Brown entered the galley, he guffawed to see Billy already at work. After some words with Tennant, Brown told Billy he could sleep on the *Eleanor Bolling* for at least Wednesday night. He checked the chart to see where men were billeted in their cabin and where there might be an extra bunk. He would see what more they could do once he conferred with Byrd.

When Billy was done washing dishes, he explored the ship properly, without fear of getting caught. One of the men showed him to a free berth near the engine room. In each room, the men who knew his face well by now waved.

Imagine trying to fall asleep amidst dogsleds and snowshoes. Men whose names he had memorized were in their bunks on his every side: flyer Ashley McKinley and chief meteorologist William Haines, who would set the day that Byrd would fly to the South Pole from their base camp on the fragile Ross Ice Barrier. Could Billy feel the heat from the engine room? The rock of any small waves?

Early the next morning, Commander Byrd arrived by train to inspect the ship and congratulate those on deck for their bravery in the storms. Before Captain Brown could speak with him about the stowaway, Byrd was off to the dock office—a quick stop before a scheduled afternoon visit to his hometown of Winchester, at the edge of the Shenandoah Valley's Blue Ridge Appalachian Mountains, for a rest in a familiar place. He still had several weeks until his own departure to the Southern Hemisphere on the whaler *Larsen*.

The three-story, high-ceiling, cream-colored Victorian manor at 326 Amherst Street was set back behind an extensive hedgerow on a brick-paved block where a strong scent of apple orchards lingered in the air. It had been constructed to Byrd's father's specifications fifty years before, a half mile from the senior Byrd's US District Attorney's office downtown. The house was covered with ivy, topped by a severely angled mansard roof with dark-green fish-scale shingles, and blessed with a wraparound verandah spiffed up by a bright yellow-and-green-striped awning. Apple trees and a large barn with stables were tucked away in the big backyard, and to the west was Darbe's Run, a small creek where Byrd and his two brothers had loved to swim. After the expedition, the colorful house would become a popular linen penny postcard: "Admiral Byrd's idyllic boyhood home."

But before Byrd could head home to his widowed mother (his father had died not long ago in 1925), a *Virginian-Pilot* reporter decided to outfox the others on the dud supply ship beat, which was considerably less interesting than anything to do with the flagship. His only real rivals were reporters for the *Norfolk Ledger-Dispatch*; the major out-of-state papers hadn't even bothered sending down anyone. Knowing that the commander was due in that day, the *Pilot*'s man found Byrd at the dock office in conference with his brother, Harry, governor of Virginia, who was in town to say hello. Governor Byrd knew the reporter well enough to call him over to meet his baby brother the explorer.

The reporter eagerly recounted the story of Billy's arrival on the ship. Byrd half listened, perplexed. Why was this reporter talking about that rapscallion again? This was old stuff, Byrd told him, mixed-up gossip from the boy's shenanigans in Brooklyn, back at the Tebo Yacht Basin the week before.

No, insisted the reporter, he was here! Really, in Virginia, for a new try. Hadn't the commander heard?

Byrd laughed hard, in a grand mood now that his missing ship had been safely moored after those horrendous storms.

Byrd hadn't known that Billy was here? The crafty newsie knew now he had a scoop—and with a bit more meddling, he could orchestrate an even better one. Wouldn't the commander like to speak to the boy?

To the reporter's delight, Byrd said yes.

The newspaperman rushed back to the *Bolling* and found Billy in the mess room with a plate of beans in his hand. Byrd wanted to see him about a possible spot! In the meantime, would he speak to the press?

Surely Billy was being ribbed. "I'm busy," he said. "They're giving me a job here, and I have to keep working."

Tennant smiled overhearing the exchange: "But maybe a new news item will help you get a berth."

Billy took the cook's advice. He told the man his name was "William Gavron," though the reporter listened knowingly, having read the New York stories—reprinted by wire service around the nation—with the kid's real name (spelling inconsistencies aside). Billy said he planned on being a mineralogist and that a trip to the Antarctic would help his career. (This was the only time Billy uttered the word *mineralogist* to the press, and it was never mentioned in his notebooks.) The reporter convinced him to pose for a photo in the *Bolling*'s galley, a picture that would run in the *Pilot* before long.

Then it was time to see Byrd and have the scary second chance to plead his case. The scene was staged at the governor's and the commander's (unnamed) dining spot near the dock. The "lucky" reporter who was orchestrating his own story jotted down that Byrd smiled at Billy and declared himself impressed by the boy's "earnestness and ambition." He'd just said he had "practically made up his mind to hire him as a mess boy," the scribe wrote, when the police arrived.

With Billy gone for the third time now, Rudy was at wit's end between Francesca's hysterics and his own fear. He'd wired the Norfolk police for information—where else could the boy be? His son had never been so far from home, not alone. Yes, he'd gone to Poland with his mother as a child and once to Washington, DC, with his class, but he'd been chaperoned. What mischief was he getting up to on his own?

After too many no-news days, Rudy took the car and headed to Virginia. Somewhere along the way, he received word by telegram that Billy had been found.

Norfolk police arrested Billy as a truant while Byrd watched. (This, despite the fact that Billy had turned eighteen days earlier, on

September 10, and was now legally an adult.) If there was a warrant out for the kid's arrest, what could he do? He didn't need bad press.

"But I'm going on that trip!" Billy told the officer on the way to the detention home where he'd be kept for the night, once again angrily (and, hopefully, with a touch of shame) waiting for his father to drive him home. He decided that he would show up at the next juncture, even if that meant hitchhiking to San Pedro, California, from where the *Larsen* would be leaving.

He was treated kindly by staff, who could see this articulate delinquent was no danger, and was escorted back to the pier for parental pick-up come morning. When Rudy arrived, the mortified father grabbed his disobedient offspring, but Billy refused to get in his father's Model A. The *Virginian-Pilot* reporter was back (Would he miss this for the world?), eavesdropping as Billy pleaded with his pop in tears, calling him sir, calling him Father, begging him to con-sider what the expedition meant to him. He loved his parents, but his mind was made up. Besides, he was an adult now—didn't his fa-ther realize? Perhaps Byrd would let him sign on without his father's permission. (Or maybe Byrd would never risk that bad press?) He was equal parts angry and terrified. Maybe Mr. Gawronski wasn't listening anymore, but the *Pilot* reporter was all ears.

Energy drained from the battle with his son, Rudy asked to speak with Captain Brown, a request swiftly granted. And then a miracle: Rudy relented.

Brown radioed Byrd, who came out to shake Rudy's hand. "A lad as persistent as you will always come out on top," he said to Billy as the boy's father looked on. Rudy was a Józef Piłsudski man, but here was a famous American aviator—a hero, the papers said—who thought highly of his good-for-nothing son. He'd been won over.

"You can be our mess boy, and I am confident you will be a good one," Byrd told the kid. There was an ear-ringing yes. Byrd laughed, adding, "I'll see you soon at New Zealand." There he would decide whether to let the kid continue on to the ice.

Billy had no time to rejoice just yet, as he was put to work lugging cargo straightaway. (He can be spotted in a press picture of the crew preparing to leave port doing just that. Perhaps the boxes were connected to a new radio generator that Byrd decreed was warranted after her original one failed in the terrifying storms off the coast.) When Rudy returned that evening to say good-bye, he had with him a telegram. News traveled fast in the modern age!

The Textile High School is proud to have one of its graduates on the Byrd expedition and knows that you will be a credit to your school and to Commander Byrd. Kindest regards from Dr. William H. Dooley, our Principal, and from all of your teachers and associates . . . Let us hear from you often.

At 5:55 p.m. on September 20, the *Eleanor Bolling* sailed for Panama with three hundred tons of supplies and twenty-eight people, including William Gregory Gawronski. The *Pilot* reporter with the juicy exclusive was there to see him off, and Billy tried to get in a word about how his narrative should be framed. "Start it off by saying my dreams have come true," he said. "I'm the happiest boy in the country! But about that other story! Do you have to put in the paper that the cops here had me?"

Aboard the ship, there was no special attention for the stowaway. For now, Billy was ordered to see Dr. Haldor Barnes: every man sailing had to be immunized for typhoid and smallpox. No kid was ever happier to get his shots. His measurements were taken so that later he could be issued clothing for the snow. They would work out how to get him the extra underwear and toiletries most stowaways couldn't be bothered to bring along.

Soon after the *Bolling* pushed off, the expedition's chief publicist, Hilton Railey, called the *Times* with the breaking news. Now the story hit big: a stowaway had been taken onto the Byrd expedition, when tens of thousands had been turned away. The *Times* pinched whole lines from the *Virginian-Pilot* article without accreditation: "My dreams have come true. No more hiding in the hold for me. I'm the happiest boy in the country."

The startling turn of events flitted through the national and even international press.

BYRD GIVES JOB TO STOWAWAY!

STOWAWAY WINS HIS GOALS TO POLE WITH BYRD!

BYRD ENLISTS NEW YORK STOWAWAY YOUTH!

The headline in New York's *Daily News* called it "The Triumph of the Century." Even *Times* adversary the *Herald Tribune* was wowed. Who cared if the story helped the *Times* circulation; it would help theirs, too. What paper could now say that Paul Siple was still *the luckiest boy of all*?

With a little nudge from a certain smooth-talking expedition publicist (the same man who had made a heroine out of Amelia Earhart), the story of Billy's astonishing pluck was picked up in Germany, Australia, Poland—even as far away as New Zealand, where people were especially eager for stories of the men soon expected on their shores. The *Dunedin Evening Star* reported that Captain Brown marveled at "the boy's dogged spirit." In London, the *Evening Telegraph* said the lad would join the rear party, or backup crew. *Poland* magazine declared the boy would go down in history "as the Kosciuszko of the Byrd Expedition." (Big praise there: every

Polish child in New York knew of Tadeusz Kosciuszko, an American Revolutionary military hero and friend of Thomas Jefferson's who had a bridge named after him in the city.)

Francesca had a lot of clipping to do after buying all the New York papers, and started yet another family scrapbook.

Rudy may have been nervous meeting Commander Byrd, but that encounter was not nearly as intimidating as going home to face the wife. Upon his return to Queens, he was, as he feared, in the doghouse. Francesca had told him to bring home her only son. That was the only thing he was supposed to do. And had he done that?

Things were so bad that a few days later Rudy hurtled past newly installed speed limit signs as they argued. The couple was too busy screaming at each other to notice, as reported by the *New York Sun* in an article headlined "Father of Polar Ship Stowaway Fined as Speeder." Magistrate Thomas F. Doyle of the Long Island City Court heard the case. Motorcycle Patrolman William Van Cleef had stopped Rudy's Model A speeding thirty-five miles per hour on Northern Boulevard, where automobilists where expected to keep to the thirty-mile-per-hour limit. Rudy pleaded guilty and begged the judge for mercy. According to the *Sun*, he offered the explanation that his wife "was shaken by her son's adventures, and he was running his wife home! He declared his wife was in 'a very upset condition,' over her son's several attempts to hide himself away on the Antarctic ships."

Magistrate Doyle was not moved and spoke sternly to Rudy. "I don't see that has any connection with the charges of speeding made against you," the stenographer recorded.

Rudy paid the $25 fine.

FIVE

SOUTH POLE OR BUST

For his first major stretch at sea, Billy was the "greenie," an easy target for pranks. *Times* auxiliary correspondent Joe de Ganahl sent the poor kid to look for green oil for the green starboard light and red oil for the portside one; Billy persisted in looking for colored oil for some time. On a rare break, the boy would sit by himself watching V formations of birds and writing letters, which he was told were to be dropped into a supposed mail buoy just beyond the surf line, to be picked up in the Gulf Stream. (The details make little sense, but alas, it took the poor newbie days to catch on.)

Forty-nine-year-old third mate Lieutenant Harry Adams was still taking notes for that book deal he hoped to score. He was five foot seven and a scrawny 136 pounds; a good Protestant with tattoos on his on chest and arms. He'd served thirty years in the navy, but unlike some of his elite armed forces peers, Adams had nothing more than a general education, though he had more of a way with character and story than those who had gone to university. He listened to people and was sure that in recording the small stuff, he got the big stuff.

Billy he sized up as "a normal loud-mouthed, fair-skin, blue-eyed, wisecracking, flapper-chasing buttinsky sort of fellow . . . a New Yorker by speech, outlook, and sophistication." The kid was getting a bit of a reputation on board as a know-it-all (though he wasn't obnoxious about it), his obsessive scrapbooking having given him all sorts of random trivia about the Antarctic climate, geography, and habitants—animal, vegetable, and mineral. He seemed restless for adventure but not especially fussy about what sort. Adams thought he "may have set out on an expedition to fight nonexistent Indians had the Byrd expedition not come to his rescue."

Restless he was. The *Bolling* sailed through the West Indies: past Haiti, past the Bahaman island of Mira Por Vos, which Billy called Voss Island in his letters home. There wasn't all that much to see—blue seas, more seas, sometimes a school of porpoises playing—and nowhere to go for a kid used to kicking around the five boroughs of New York on his own. It was hot, too—hot enough that the men would walk on deck naked to feel the breeze, until the sudden Caribbean rains sent them scampering to the cramped hold below.

The brutalities of seafaring life are not always the waves. There are arguments, the snorers, the disgusting personal hygiene. There are those who control the radio and the phonograph, and fights over what music will be heard. That is, if there is a station, and pity the man forever trying to pick up a signal from the Caribbean islands they passed.

When Billy's letters did make it home—mailed weeks later, when the ship docked in Panama—they were tinged with surprising melancholy. "The reason that my writing and wording is poor is because of

the ships rolling and because they're all joking around me," he wrote
his parents, not mentioning that rich daddy's boys like de Ganahl
made him the butt of their jokes. His letters showed a jarring mix of
his old silly, go-lucky attitude and a new seriousness—almost a sense
of regret. In one particularly wistful letter to Rudy and Francesca,
he wrote:

> *I am of course very homesick and wish I could go home when
> we reach Panama, but I want to stick it out, to show them
> that I want to be a man . . . [I'm] improving morally as well as
> physically. Haven't even had time to bite my nails! I hope that
> you are all well and happy, as I can tell you frankly I wish I
> were home.*

This explorer business wasn't all it was chalked up to be.

It was all ashore October 4 at Cristóbal, on the Atlantic Ocean side
of the Panama Canal. The *Bolling*, as the *New York Times* put it,
was "scarcely bigger than a tugboat," and dwarfed by freighters
and oil tankers. It entered the locks heavily laden with coal. At port,
every man raced off board except for the unlucky four left on watch.
Cristóbal was well known to mail-deprived and sex-starved sailors,
and the shore-going men—letters from home waiting for them in
duffels onshore—knew exactly what they would spend their pocket
money on: for some, opiates; and for most, prostitutes the seamen
called *putas*, who waited on the dock to do business with the randy
crew, including the eminent academics on board. Longtime sailors
were wiser than that, racing in hungry packs to the crooked, narrow
streets of "wet" Colón, just blocks away. (Cristóbal was "dry," part
of the American territory leased from Panama for 999 years.) Mar-
ried men might have stopped at flirtation and the American-style

partner dancing the local ladies had mastered from watching motion pictures, but rare was discretion after so many weeks at sea. Billy, not the virgin his mother thought he was, likely joined in with some of the money his father had slipped him in Virginia. But if he did, his experiences on land were wisely not chronicled in letters home.

With a post office in Cristóbal, now was a chance for drunken crew members to send private love letters instead of Radiograms via the official shipboard radio that were received over shortwave radio and transcribed and printed, like a telegram. They were managed by the Expedition, so were fair game for any *Times* article, if a great way to save money on stamps. Maybe one thought to send a more private letter to Sunshine.

Seamen with beery breath were late reboarding the ship after "toot stops" at Colón's dance parlors and cantinas such as Over the Top and the Atlantic Café. With a wink, Harry Adams coded dodgy behavior for his readers, writing: "We were but men and of the so-called 'he' variety—we did very little singing in the choir . . . [and] had more than a dash of whoopee." By his account, everyone took part in the fun except for one bluenosed sailor who stayed on board reading the Bible. George Tennant, the *Bolling*'s cook and Billy's first friend, later recalled his crewmates being treated to an arena fight between a bull and four tigers, ending, he added salaciously, in death for all creatures except the men of the Expedition.

Captain Brown caught up with Captain Melville in Cristóbal. With both the *City of New York* and the *Eleanor Bolling* briefly in harbor together, men were shuffled on paper and a few switched ships to fill open spots. A low-level seaman on the *New York* slipped on the wet deck and sprained his back, and a twenty-three-year-old coal passer on the *Bolling* was sent home to Ohio with a sinus infection, even after pleading with Byrd. His illness was not contagious, and he had served three weeks without complaint, but the expedition physician was not taking any chances of a crew member falling seriously ill at sea.

Billy was offered his first promotion: from mess boy to a coal passer in the Black Gang, the nickname for the unfortunate souls in the fire room who worked stripped to the waist and drenched in sweat in tedious shifts of four hours on and eight off. One of the ship's coal passers, and already a good friend, was the witty twenty-six-year-old ex-marine corporal Charles "Kess" Kessler from Washington, DC, who had served with Byrd on his North Pole trip and was somewhat cavalier about his rough and largely unappreciated days below the equator, wiring home: "We almost lost our coal (overboard), [and] when the weather is rough, you have to do the Charleston to say upright."

Billy was hesitant to leave the sanctuary of the galley, but Tennant told him to man up: Byrd would notice big-time if he accepted an unpleasant assignment in the grubby, hot stokehold. "Byrd will notice" were magic words. And, indeed, having the stowaway in the fire room eased any qualms that the boy was getting off too easy. Billy was back on the commander's radar, and, just like in a Horatio Alger tale, a good kid pulling his weight after all.

There were two new crew members on the *New York*, one of them Lyle Womack, a former electronics salesman married to silent-film actress and aviatrix Ruth Elder, who for a time held the long-distance record for a flight by a woman. Heartbroken that the "Miss America of Aviation" refused to kiss him when she returned to New York for a tickertape parade after her nearly completed transatlantic flight (an oil leak forced an emergency landing), Womack had fled, lovelorn, to the Canal Zone, where until the Byrd crew came to town, he had been doing odd jobs for his father, a whisky manufacturer. Womack filed for divorce on September 6, 1928, in Balboa. Elder did not contest it.

Three new passengers were also added to the *Bolling*: six-week-old mutt puppies Jack and Col, and Rex, a waterfront bulldog who took to Chief Engineer Frank "Mac" McPherson and followed the Scottish sailor up the plank and into the boiler room, where the dog was renamed Bum. Billy missed his own dog, Tootsie, something terrible and was glad to have more animals aboard.

The *City of New York* was the first of the two ships to leave Cristóbal, heading westward through the canal to the Pacific Ocean port of Balboa. (Reports claimed the departure was delayed because of Panama Canal levies that Byrd had forgotten to pay, with the necessary funds eventually secured from Montgomery Ward heir George Thorne, who fronted the expedition hundreds of dollars he pulled from his pocket.) The eight-hour passage was a safe stretch, though the journey through the fabled Panama Canal was thrilling to the novice adventurers among the thirty-two men on board. The prior weekend, the whaler *Sir James Clark Ross*, with its ninety-seven sledge huskies and malamutes, had taken its turn.

As the *New York* reached Balboa, word arrived that Byrd had come to a decision about Bob Lanier, the black stowaway. From the day he set sail, Bob had faced bigotry from the *New York*'s crew. Several men, some of whom would go on to don blackface for entertainment, were open about their displeasure that a "darkie" was along for the journey, sharing their glory. They had Captain Melville's ear, and the cantankerous Melville informed Byrd that the man who had once crossed the country alone had no "sea legs."

Byrd contacted executives at United Fruit Company, which had supplied the ships with bananas for publicity; many of the men on board would for decades associate their polar journey with the noxious sweetness of overripe bananas. Bob Lanier was sent eastward to Cristóbal, where he was shipped off to New York on the

United Fruit liner SS *Ulua*. For Byrd, a top officer's loyalty was more important than letting Lanier make black history.

A reporter at the influential black paper the *New York Age* tracked down Lanier upon his return, publishing a sympathetic article in which Lanier attested that he had been treated unfairly and would probably appeal his dismissal to New Jersey's governor, A. Harry Moore. He had signed on to the ship at a salary of one cent per month—the same pay as most of the crew—and with his name still on the rolls, he remained legally a member of the expedition.

Though Byrd's ships were leaving the Americas, they were far from out of the American public's mind. Coverage back home was still going strong; sure, there were not as many front-page headlines, but newspaper readers were still offered almost daily reports, especially by Byrd's sponsor the *New York Times*. And while Billy didn't know it until he received a wire from his parents, New York's many papers now ran semiregular bulletins on the local hero's progress, typified by one printed in the *Flushing Journal* on October 6:

BAYSIDE BOY WITH BYRD TELEGRAPHS FATHER HERE

Mr. Rudolf Gawronski received this first telegram at 40-21 First Street, Bayside:

Nearly through the Panama Canal now. Wish I could be with you, Dad. But it's the South Pole or Bust.

The stopover in Cristóbal seemed to have considerably improved the boy's mood.

Captain Brown's supply ship arrived in Balboa the next day under an overcast sky. After being held for three days over unpaid levies, the *Bolling*'s lines were cast off, and the ship, with Billy in his new and physically exhausting job in the coal room, left port once again just before three o'clock in the afternoon, piled high with six hundred tons of coal. The next stop was not for another 4,300 miles: Tahiti.

On the same date, October 10, Byrd, after a few days' delay ridding himself of a nasty cold and an alarming temperature of 102, left San Pedro aboard the extraordinarily large whaling steamship *C. A. Larsen*. Thousands of spectators crowded round as ten thousand tons of cargo were loaded on the ship, including seventy-five sheep for meat and a dozen milch cows, joining seven breeding pigs, six bleating goats, and a grunting boar. While one report had the livestock headed to Antarctica, the animals were more likely destined for another land after the expedition disembarked in New Zealand. In either case, it was surely loud in the animal hold.

Bernt Balchen, Harold June, Dean C. Smith, and Alton Parker—the dazzling flyboys who would soon share Byrd's fame for their polar exploits—joined the commander on the whaler. The pilots had it easy; Byrd wanted them rested. Also aboard were the remaining aircraft and the eldest member of the crew: sixty-seven-year-old Martin Ronne, the Norwegian sail master who had wintered over with Amundsen back in the heroic age, sewing the tent he would leave behind at the Pole.

The expedition was sprouting stowaways now. Two days after leaving California, two boys, encouraged by Billy's widely reported success, were found aboard the *Larsen* four hundred miles out to sea. The total count of stowaways who boarded was now five—six if you counted Sunshine. Captain Oscar Nilsen, a soft-spoken Norwegian-born veteran of the sea, was unfazed; as reported to papers, he chortled over the matter with the commander. Once he reached New Zealand, Nilsen gently let the boys go into American consulate hands; they did not impress Byrd enough for him to keep them on past the city of Wellington.

The stretch between the Panama Canal and the coaling stop at Tahiti was nearly a month, an arduous and dull chunk of time at sea. Partly to kill time, Billy sent Radiograms to his parents; he had been promoted again from lowly coal passer to second fireman (fire stoker). Although he no longer had to be at everyone's beck and call—supplying coal to the firemen or wiping the engine room decks—he was still down there in the steaming heat, tending to the fire, shoveling coal, and watching water levels. It was tough manual labor, and he bragged it was making him hard as nuts. He always ended the Radiograms by asking Rudy and Francesca to send Babcia his love. Billy also found time to wire his neighborhood firemen at Bayside's Hook and Ladder 152, the ones he used to pester.

As news from abroad trickled back to Bayside, the *Flushing Journal* continued to report on the new Patron Saint of Plucky Kids, even tracking down Rudy in his home for a parent's take: "Father predicted he would be dropped off in New Zealand if not applying himself. He took turns at heaving ash and clove clinkers—everyone admired him." It was probably best that the other men on board didn't know the media was playing favorites. They teased Billy enough, even if he was growing less of a greenhorn by the day, toughing it out without complaint.

By the sixteenth, the *Times* had the position of the *Bolling* by wireless: 270 miles northwest of the Galápagos Islands, latitude 2 degress 35 minutes north, longitude 95.5 west. She crossed the equator two days later, just before noon on a breezy, sunshiny day with a surprisingly low temperature of 71 degrees Fahrenheit. Passing the equator came with rites of passage for first-timers, and fifteen men were initiated into the whimsical Order of Neptune that day. The inductees included eminent geologist Professor Laurence Gould, third in command on the expedition; strikingly handsome aerial surveyor Ash McKinley, often photographed in aviation goggles and

buttery-brown aviator jacket; Clair "Alec" Alexander, the edgy supply officer nobody dared mess with; and Harvard class of '25 *Times*
auxiliary correspondent and former coal passer Joe de Ganahl, who
had long before been promoted to second mate.

At one thirty in the afternoon, a whistle sounded on deck, and
there emerged, in great nautical tradition, King Neptune and his
queen, portrayed by two Swedish seamen: third mate William Erickson and a good-natured and wiry fireman named George Sjo-
gren. Lieutenant Harry Adams, assigned as the scribe, read to the
gathered: "In the name of Rex Neptune, Supreme Ruler of the seas
within the polar boundaries of the North and the Great Antarctic of
the South, I greet you and command your attention."

But two would-be inductees were missing: William Gawronski
and his coal passer pal Kess, who had been with Byrd to the North
Pole but had never passed this far south. Billy had shinnied high up
the aftermast (the mast nearest the stern) and was ordered down by
Captain Brown, who joked he would otherwise shoot the boy with
one of the rifles on board. Kess was found ten minutes later, hanging
over the ship's stern. He was given "the works": head shave, getting
dunked in a barrel, and being pelted with mustard pies and roast
squid George Tennant had prepared for the ceremony.

The *Times* coverage made no mention of additional punishment
doled out to Billy. Only later, with the publication of Harry Adams's
memoir, would the more scandalous details of initiation day be revealed: Billy was ordered to pull down his pants to check if the man
with the Polish name was a Jew and not, as he claimed, a Catholic.
Many New York hospitals at the time encouraged circumcision for
health reasons, and despite Babcia's Virgin Mary around the boy's
neck, he was found guilty. Billy was secretly horrified but played
along.

For weeks now, there'd been ribbing galore over on the *City of*

New York for the real Jew of the Byrd expedition: airplane mechanic Bennie Roth, one of the shortest crew members at five foot three. By one sailor's account, no one on the flagship went ten minutes without telling a Jewish joke at Roth's expense. Like most victims of prejudice in this era, Roth tried to laugh it off. There was no record of his punishment by the *City of New York*'s scribe of the Ancient Order of Neptune, Russell Owen, when the flagship passed the equator. (Hopefully, he too didn't have to pull his pants down to show his "crime" of circumcision.)

The giant *Larsen* passed the equator three days after the *Bolling*, and since this was Commander Byrd's first crossing, he was not spared the maritime ritual. Perhaps because Captain Nilsen's wife was aboard—sharing her husband's cabin and helping with the logbooks, as many whaling-ship wives did—things did not get as uninhibited. Still, Byrd was dunked in a tank constructed on the upper forecastle deck. The commander, so careful to control his narrative, was not going to let anyone say in print that he wasn't a team player.

After a day of festivities, it was back to weeks of monotonous open sea. Fortunately, Byrd had prearranged for lectures to alleviate the welter of sameness. On the *City of New York*, Captain Melville was photographed teaching astronomy. On the *Bolling*, Billy learned about classical music, finally understanding his father's pride in Chopin's contributions to Romanticism. (After the trip, he would start to build a classical collection of his own.) Ukulele Dick was, as promised, good for daily entertainment, and those who could sing sang. All distractions were welcome.

Some took to playing cards in the midship saloon. During one poker game with Gould, Tennant, and budding gambler Billy at the table, a large flying fish eleven inches long and twelve across soared through a porthole ten feet above the waterline. The twitching fish struck one of the players on the shoulder and flopped onto the center of the table. Billy laughed his head off—it would become a favorite story from the expedition—and Tennant quipped, "It will be served for breakfast tomorrow." It was the first of several fish to fly into the saloon.

Several classes were set up to prepare the men for the Antarctic mission. One course on radiotelegraphy was cotaught by former North Pole stowaway Malcolm Hanson, the chief radio engineer, and Howard Mason, another operator. Together they would attempt the longest-distanced radio signals to date (communicating with a station in Norway) and, most important, keep track of Byrd on his flight over the South Pole. The commander, Hanson reminded all, was a stickler for safety who required every last sailor to know radio code; Billy dutifully attended the radiotelegraphy classes twice a week. In between lessons, he read books recommended by Laurence Gould and the other eminent scientists on board, including one on Darwin, which, he remembered later, changed some of the views his pious father had drummed into him. Even the less educated sailors found themselves reading scientific texts and fine literature.

Despite his first hoorahs reciting poetry back in Polish school on the Lower East Side, Billy was embarrassed not to know which one was Yeats and which one was Keats. He resolved to remedy this hole in his education when he returned to America.

The days dragged on. A lot of nothing goes on between ports, and back in New York at expedition headquarters, press maven Hilton Railey realized that Billy came in handy now. A stowaway maturing into a fine young sailor was a good story with which to snag short attention spans. He made sure Billy's telegrams to his parents were published in all the region's papers, even the most innocuous stuff: "Overjoyed with your message back. I shall expect them often . . . I will send you a long one from Tahiti! Your loving son." Mass plays and niche plays: Byrd was mass, and the Gawronski kid was niche. To his surprise, Railey found there was national interest in how the novelty stowaway was faring, and his people started asking Captain Brown for anecdotes about how the loveable scoundrel was shaping up at sea. Railey fed stowaway stories to the New Zealand papers, too—a wise move, as goodwill would be needed there soon. Miles away, from Auckland to Christchurch, Billy Gawronski was becoming a household name.

Meanwhile, the other boy wonder, Paul Siple, was having a miserable time over on the *City of New York*, where curmudgeon Captain Melville had no patience for such nonsense as a Boy Scout on his ship. Melville seemed to take pleasure in making life wretched for Siple, always finding him extra demeaning tasks. (Paul Siple, as an older man, recalled Melville inexplicably raging when someone on board opened a can of powdered milk called Klim; his crew members promptly nicknamed him Captain Klim.)

On October 28 the *Bolling* crew saw land again as the ship passed five miles to the south of the Disappointment Islands. On deck and straining hard for a sight of any of the supposed two hundred natives, they were sorely disappointed indeed.

Tahiti! The *Bolling* arrived on November 1, with the *City of New York* pulling into the Tahitian capital of Papeete, an exotic French-speaking city of three thousand residents, only hours behind. A few of the men were old friends and climbed the rails to greet one another, slapping backs. While Captains Melville and Brown could exchange the occasional message via wire service or Morse code, their crews were not always privy to their plans. With the *City of New York* scheduled to refuel in Pago Pago, American Samoa, the men had not expected to meet up until New Zealand.

The residents of Tahiti had enjoyed a considerable amount of contact with sailors on American ships since the opening of the

Panama Canal in 1914; the nation had become a regular refueling spot for commercial vessels and tourist boats. The government had recently extended Papeete's wharf to permit two large ships to dock side by side, and it actively wooed US dollars and trade.

Certainly the members of the Byrd expedition were wooed, and in a far more forward fashion. By one sailor's account, native ladies dropped their brightly colored cotton dresses and swam naked to the ships. Billy was smitten. "I had quite a hectic day in Papeete," he wrote his father, asking him to use discretion when quoting from his letter to others. "I am ashamed to say but it was due to the girls."

That evening, an expatriate living in Papeete, one Mrs. Miller, gave a party against the wishes of the American consul, for she was damned if the US government was going to extend Prohibition to French Polynesia. By Harry Adams's account, she was aided by a "south seas princess in silk pajamas." Other native beauties poured champagne donated by the French crew of the Chicopee cruise line, which was also invited to the party.

Billy fell in with some locals who wanted to show him the town. Just a skip from the waterfront were fifteen saloons with dance floors, automatic player pianos, and drinks aplenty: beer and French champagne. And the dancing! As Billy surreptitiously wrote his father: "Oh! I just felt happy . . . I danced with one of the fair beauties to holy hell, and the local people were amazed to see an American boy keeping time with experienced dancers." He gave no indication whether the dancing was modern or traditional, but it was clearly uninhibited.

Not that all the expedition members enjoyed themselves among the local population. Paul Siple wrote in his journals that he was disappointed the local women were "flabby and flat-faced"—words that could never have flowed from urbanite Billy's pen. Siple preferred the local wildlife, with journal entries on spiny sea urchins and "hundreds of rainbow-colored fish, the size of a pet goldfish."

The following night—far too soon—the *Bolling* left the raucous island at eleven fifteen, headed now for New Zealand. The *City of New York* set sail the next evening. Both ships took with them coconuts, which the cooks would use for favorite American desserts such as coconut cream pie and custards; there was also a replenished stock of bananas as those donated by United Fruit back in Panama were long ago eaten.

According to a wired account from Billy's stokehold friend Kess, an unofficial race to New Zealand began when the *Bolling* zipped past the *City of New York* en route from Tahiti. The contest made for a chunky *New York Times* story but cannot have been constructed purely for the public, as many men aboard both ships mentioned it excitedly in their journals.

As the crew of the *Bolling* left the tropical seas, temperatures dropped to the 30s. There would be no more equatorial sunshine for nearly two years—at least not for the lucky men picked to winter over. Billy hoped he was still in consideration for that honor. Byrd had yet to make clear exactly how many men would make the cut, but certainly a stowaway was not a high priority. How could he prove his worth?

Byrd arrived in Wellington, on the unusually windy southwestern tip of New Zealand's North Island, the first week of November. By the 1920s, the country had close to one and a half million inhabitants between both main islands, and while the hilly landscape and rugged coastline seemed a little otherworldly, the adoring ladies hanging out on the docks in packs—ladies who had been reading the expedition members' names for months now, and who were, Harry Adams would note, "not one whit less powdered or lip-sticked than their sisters in New York"—were pleasingly familiar. Everything

American, fawned over in magazines and much discussed on radio, was in. When the Byrd party reached town, hitting the streets with jackets and ties that had been packed back in New York, they were surprised that on the other side of the world the architectural rage was California-style concrete bungalows with low-pitched roofs, large overhangs, and simple porches. Governor-general Sir Charles Fergusson's wife, Lady Alice Mary Fergusson, had bobbed her hair like a Hollywood starlet. Wellington prided itself on being a modern city, changing with the times.

Byrd disembarked from the *Larsen* to enormous crowds. While Kiwis were fairly inured to European explorers leaving their ports for the southernmost continent, these Americans aroused curiosity. They were from the land that had invented gramophones and silent cinema! The commander was given an official greeting by Premier Joseph G. Coates at the capital (two days later, it must be said—Byrd wasn't quite the priority he was in the States). There he was presented with a Maori robe by, as the American papers put it, wowed by the exoticism, a "full-blooded" indigenous Maori: Sir Maui Pomare, minister of internal affairs.

Reporters stateside took to peppering their stories with New Zealand trivia: Did readers know that Australian Gabriel Read discovered gold near Dunedin in 1861 in a gully that now bore his name, sparking the Otago gold rush? Did they know that New Zealand had more than five hundred war memorials honoring the country's eighteen thousand soldiers, known colloquially as "diggers," lost in the Great War?

The Kiwi public was very much aware of all things Antarctica; the prominent men who greeted Byrd even filled him in on an Australian expedition that was just getting under way. Had he heard of it? Oh yes, Byrd let on without revealing his inner distress. Just as Scott, Shackleton, and Amundsen saw one another as rivals earlier in the century, Byrd now had his very own archrival in the mechanical age: Hubert Wilkins. In a spectacular display of corporate rivalry, American William Randolph Hearst (who owned twenty-eight papers, including the *New York American*, the *New York Evening Journal*, the *Chicago Herald and Examiner*, and the *Los Angeles Examiner*), wanting to one-up the *Times*, had offered the forty-year-old Aussie $25,000 (big money then) to become the first man to fly over the South Pole, in what would surely be known to history as the Wilkins-Hearst Expedition. Hearst, the bully model for Orson Welles's *Citizen Kane*, was synonymous with yellow journalism. He had already been vilified for provoking the Spanish-American War twenty years before, so a little matter like sabotaging his own country's chances of going down in the annals of Antarctic exploration may not have weighed much on his conscience.

Not that Hearst had acknowledged his aims publicly. Wilkins had announced that he did not plan to fly across the pole but keep to a study of Antarctica's Graham Land: the northernmost section of the Antarctic Peninsula; the part of the continent closest to South America. Still, there had been some printed reports that Hearst had pledged $100,000 if his man beat Byrd to the South Pole. Byrd was asked if he was nervous, but he publicly cheered on his rival. Who knew the truth? In any case, Kiwi officials assured Byrd that his expedition was the one New Zealanders cared about, perhaps because he was bringing attention to their fair cities. Byrd's flight was the one the majority of Americans cared about, too, despite William Randolph Hearst's best efforts to ignore Byrd in his papers. Wilkins was Australian. Byrd was an American. It was a patriotic age.

While Byrd was feted onshore, things were rougher going for the men stuck on the *Bolling*. Way back during the first Atlantic Ocean swells, the men had nicknamed her the "*Evermore Rolling*," and 550 miles north of Dunedin—during an even more ferocious storm—she had lived up to her name once again by rolling and pitching excessively. On November 13 the *Bolling* crossed the international date line, and four days later, two months after leaving New York, she reached Wellington at last. Although Byrd was already in town, there was a heartwarming reception for the *Bolling* men at the dock, but the supply ship was quickly in and out, picking up cargo from the *Larsen*—which would not be making the journey to Antarctica—before continuing on her overloaded way down to Dunedin, on the South Island, from which she would leave for the icy frontier.

The *Bolling* reached Dunedin the next day, Sunday, November 18, mooring early morning within city limits at the Rattray Street Wharf, a small port happily near local homes and hotels with real baths and, above all, dames. Settled by Scots in 1848, its name Gaelic for Edinburgh, Dunedin was New Zealand's largest city, although with all of eighty-five thousand residents, it was still a somewhat sleepy place, with a distinct architecture of bluestone bricks that would still be the pride of the city nearly a century later. The larger port in town, Port Chalmers, was the third most important in the Southern Hemisphere.

The Sabbath was taken seriously in these parts, and despite the "modern look" girls everywhere, Sunday blue laws were strictly enforced. So while there was no official reception, hundreds of people personably welcomed the *Bolling* men at the piers. Conveniently for the unexpected celebrities, New Zealand had repealed its Prohibition law four days before, and in private homes, the liquor flowed legally—a celebration that continued in the pubs as soon as Monday came.

Happy drinkers told Billy that he was already well known thanks to a front-page article that had run nationally: a cheat sheet about the most colorful Yanks arriving soon on Kiwi shores. Was this a joke? The eighteen-year-old had no idea he'd been all over

New Zealand's newspapers. Someone handed him a clipping, which he mailed home proudly: "Not the least important person on the boat is William Gavronski, whose birthplace is given as New York City. Adventure seems to be the very breath of life to this boy." (They misspelled his name in New Zealand, too.)

Rudy and Francesca had sent mail ahead to Dunedin's poste restante. Opening a promisingly thick envelope, Billy pocketed some much-needed American dollars to exchange and read his father's enclosed note: "Have you got enough money? Probably you have bought a camera, but let us know how you are. Feet and nose? Did you get shoes for yourself in New Zealand?" Rudy knew the expedition was not paying his son.

With no spare funds in his pocket other than what he'd just been sent, Billy did not have enough for new shoes, let alone a sailor's dance. He owed people money lent to him in Tahiti. But the stowaway soon found he could dine out on those paragraphs in the paper. Starstruck girls vied to gain the eye of the "Happiest Boy in America" and maybe even invite him home for dinner. Curious locals were all too happy to let the Americans into their homes.

The all-star dogs were almost as popular as the men. Dunediners flocked to the *Sir James Clark Ross*, which had made port in October, to see Klondike legend Arthur Walden and his ninety-six specially bred Labradors. (One developed an abscess on its throat during the voyage and was thrown overboard.) The canines had arrived looking sickly, but after Dunedin's top veterinarians fiddled with their dog formula, they soon made a remarkable recovery in the fresh air. Locals turned out in droves to be photographed with Chinook, the elder statesman of the pack dogs, and Skookun Siwash, an "Indian dog" of wolfish strain, who caught their collective fancy in popular stories on radio and in the papers. The Kiwis paid a shilling each for their visits, which added up to real money, as everyone in town, it seemed, was headed to the docks for a look. The tidy sum went toward Byrd's diminished business account.

Dunedin journalists, meanwhile, proudly reminded the American visitors that their town offered recreational choices such as checkers, chess, baseball, amateur boxing, and quoits, a game similar to horseshoes but involving rubber rings being tossed. No one could complain of boredom, though after weeks at sea, most of the crew members found something to do with themselves in the boozy, cheery environment besides box. Several sexual relationships would have surprising longevity, with one dockside hookup resulting in an unexpected child for a *Bolling* oiler.

Amidst the revelry, there were also rattled nerves. Byrd still had yet to decide which of the men he would take to the ice and which would wait out the expedition in New Zealand. Crew members could be excused for getting jittery.

One man's behavior, however, was downright strange. Dick Brophy, the expedition's second in command and Byrd's business manager, had begun acting oddly on the voyage through the Pacific, firing off incoherent telegrams to crew members' wives and sweethearts and causing a disturbance with his garbled speech and paranoiac ramblings. The straitjackets that Byrd had theatrically put on board each boat to be "prepared as a Boy Scout" suddenly didn't seem so laughable. The commander now ordered Brophy to remain in New Zealand at a desk job, replacing him with well-liked geologist Laurence Gould, a safer bet. Brophy would ultimately wheedle his way into going to the ice, although his erratic behavior would cause him to be quickly sent back to New Zealand, where he would be arrested as a public nuisance and offered a stay in a sanitarium or a one-way ticket home, which he would take. In New York, he would check into the infamous Bellevue Medical Hospital for the insane. Most officially sanctioned books on the expedition skip over this drama, saying only that Brophy stayed on in New Zealand because he was overwhelmed with paperwork. There was considerable whitewashing of unpleasant facts for fear of crossing Byrd.

To the great surprise of all, the expedition added a last-minute member: volunteer Vaclav Vojtech, a gifted Czech geologist. Although the man spoke little English, he had traveled to New Zealand at his own cost in hopes of talking his way on board. And Vojtech was in luck: with Gould taking over as second in command, Byrd had suddenly found himself down one geologist. In a Czech newspaper interview printed after he was miraculously accepted onto the crew, Vojtech mentioned getting on well with a talky stowaway named Billy. "The sea gave him a good school," he said, "and I believe that the kid became a man."

Billy certainly tried to be a good son, making up for his past sins. Reminded frequently that he was all his parents and grandmother had to live for, he dutifully sent letters home from Oceania, slipping in clean-living details about a visit to a Polish home in town—no word on whether the Polish home housed an attractive Polish daughter—and historical notes on the Poles who'd come to New Zealand in the 1870s to drain swamps, fell trees, and build a railway system for the new colony. Many went on to own their own farms, especially on the South Island.

After a quick jaunt to Wellington to load up on food and fuel, the *Bolling* returned to Dunedin to meet up with the men of the newly arrived *City of New York*. It was the last chance for outings. Suave pilot Dean Smith told a local reporter that he'd spent the greatest day fishing, even if the residents who took him out on their boat were disappointed. Six-pounders were tossed back! In this part of the world, his hosts had told him, fifteen trout a day up to twelve pounds each was the norm.

While the men enjoyed their last pleasant days of civilization, the massive whaler *Ross*, hired only for the Pacific journey, shoved off on a profitable whaling expedition. By 1928, this had become a highly mechanized operation that used ammunition to blow up trapped animals, hardly the romantic harpooning Billy had read about in *Moby-Dick*. The technological "advances" of the early twentieth century made it all too easy to kill, and forty thousand whales in the Antarctic were converted to oil annually.

Byrd, meanwhile, was still stuck in Wellington, ensnarled by official duties. With all the press that Hilton Railey had arranged, the explorer was now almost as well known there as he was back home. He did have genuine enthusiasm for his November 20 meeting with Sir Douglas Mawson, a legendary heroic age explorer and British-born Australian who'd turned down a spot on Robert Scott's iconic expedition aboard the ship *Terra Nova* in order to lead his own adventure in 1912. Mawson was the sole survivor of a dramatic sledging outing with huskies over ice, walking frostbitten to his rescue. Byrd claimed he was giddy to meet his idol, and that the aging explorer's 1915 book *The Home of the Blizzard* was the Antarctica Bible as far as he was concerned. Afterward, Byrd had a packed Rotary Club to attend to, bringing howdys from his fellow American Rotarians. At the meeting's end, the exhausted commander joined in for a rousing round of "For He's a Jolly Good Fellow" to close out the evening.

On the same night, against all odds, twenty-year-old former stowaway Bob Lanier set sail across the Pacific toward Auckland, having talked his way onto the freighter *Golden State*, as a mess boy. It had been a crazy five-week journey to San Francisco, much of it made by foot, with occasional lifts from drivers willing (astonishingly, in a Jim Crow era) to take him a few hours closer to California. Bob prayed he would get to New Zealand in time to plead his case with Byrd. He could wash dishes during the wintering over, maybe even see the South Pole. Who could deny his perseverance? He had almost lost his life twice on the way to San Francisco, once in a blizzard in Wyoming and then in the heat of the Nevada desert. South Pole or bust.

The following week, the Dunedin crowds cheered Byrd at the train station when he arrived from Wellington's pomp and ceremony, done with his North Island duties and ready to focus on his coming months on ice. He transferred his snowshoes and fur coat to the *City of New York*. Two days later, he announced to the crew that no one would be left behind in New Zealand. Everyone would go to Antarctica and work hard to set up the first village on ice; only then would he select the wintering-over party to stay for the next eighteen months.

Behind the scenes, the seamen built alliances. They understood keenly that there would be fame for anyone who wintered over with Byrd. Of course, the top officers and scientists would be asked to stay. But who else? Billy desperately wanted to overwinter, but so did Byrd's "orderly": the winning Boy Scout, de facto competition in the "one for the kids" slot. Billy and Paul Siple knew they couldn't both stay over, as neither was especially useful, although either choice would make for great publicity. As least Siple had Byrd's ear until they got to the Ross Ice Barrier: he was now assigned to the same ship as Byrd, the *New York*, while Billy was slated to remain on the *Bolling*.

All would be decided, Byrd promised as they prepared to raise anchor on New Zealand's shores, the crews saying their good-byes to lovers and drinking buddies. Early on the morning of December 2, the *Eleanor Bolling* and the *City of New York* left Dunedin together. To Antarctica!

SIX

FIRST ICE

Word was radioed to the *Bolling* that a New Zealander stowaway had been found aboard the *City of New York* right out of the harbor: a silver-haired senior who had been to Antarctica before and whose spirit of polar adventure was reawakened, inspired in part by Billy's stowaway success. This seventh stowaway of the trip was placed aboard a tug and returned to Dunedin's Port Chalmers. Billy was heavily ribbed: look what he did now, inspiring grandpas!

So close to their destination, Byrd had no patience for detours. He instructed the captains at his command to head straight to the barrier, bypassing the famous Mount Erebus, an active volcano, and the penguin rookery at Cape Adare on the mouth of the Ross Sea; the west coast of the Ross Ice Shelf was too out of the way. Even by the most direct route of 2,350 miles, their voyage could take several days with bad weather conditions. Some adventure nuts, particularly the well-read scientists, were sorely disappointed to miss the volcano that had figured so prominently in Shackleton's and Scott's journeys. And Cape Adare was the site of historic huts built for Norwegian explorer Carsten Borchgrevink, whose 1899 expedition under the British flag launched the heroic age. Borchgrevink and his crew were the first to overwinter on the continent, with ninety Siberian dogs huddled outside the crew's small shed. Captain Brown determined privately to swing by the site if he ever had a chance.

The crew was squished in for this stage of the passage, its ships overstuffed with freight and extra men from the *Ross* and the *Larsen*. There were twenty-nine men now on the *Bolling* and fifty-four on the *New York*, with more than a hundred dogs divided between the two. (Fifteen more had been purchased in New Zealand, for around £400 a head, when the original dogs had taken ill.) In such cramped quarters, the ship's complement quickly gave up any notion of personal space, even if there were fewer duties now with extras on board.

After a gentle start, the weather turned. Day by day, the temperature dropped. *Times* reporter Russell Owen was seasick—small wonder, with twenty- to twenty-five-foot-high waves tearing down on the ships. Being above deck meant walking around wet and freezing cold; their polar parkas were hardly waterproof. Water leaked down to lower levels, often drenching precious letters. The ship reeked of wet dogs and too many men and occasional vomit. Billy, miraculously not too ill, wondered what it would take for them to capsize.

Owen sent word of his plight to the *Times*'s headquarters by the secret simple letter substation code he had worked out with his editors for all his messages; Byrd was a notorious control freak. Byrd, too, wrote in code to prevent potential saboteurs, leaving a master deciphering sheet with his publicity department in New York. Little did Owen know he was being written about in Byrd's cryptic dispatches: the commander carped that the star reporter was not writing what he ought to—namely, glowing stories about Byrd. As the ships inched toward Antarctica, a worrisome coded message came back from expedition headquarters: PR man Hilton Railey was out for a few days with a bad case of herpes. The note added, "Not to worry."

And still the ships hardly moved. In a new plan, the *New York*'s hawser, a thick rope used for mooring, was fastened to the *Bolling*'s stern. Tied together, the boats could now make seven knots, or roughly eight miles per hour. "A sailing ship in tow of a steamship!" Owen managed to exclaim in a short note printed back in New York.

Billy, surprised he had found his sea legs after a few initial days of queasiness, was often on deck on breaks from the stokehold, even in the storms. Captain Brown was surprised how well the kid fared in rough waters. All was officially exciting again as they approached the frozen continent, and Billy kept his eyes peeled for sights such as Saint Elmo's fire: mysterious balls of discharged electricity that supposedly clung to prominent points on ships (like their masts), and were said to be a common phenomenon in Antarctic waters.

Navy-trained Harry Adams could be found above board in his polar parka, too. He viewed Billy less as a curiosity now and more as a chum. They all had their cliques. Adams had a special rapport with Byrd's thirty-five-year-old secretary and now shipboard personnel officer, Charley Lofgren, an even-keeled former navy man like him who had transferred from the whaler *Larsen* to the *Bolling* back in New Zealand. Lofgren, who had recently learned his mother had died, appreciated Adams's light banter. One brightly lit night close to the Antarctic Circle on midwatch, the men sat puffing Chesterfields, taking in the smell of the salt air, having a gam on deck. Lofgren pointed to something pink in the distance. Adams blinked, sure it was a pink whale. "No doubt about it!"

Billy strolled by, bringing coffee from the galley. Asked for his opinion on the pink whale, which Adams declared loudly to be the king of the whales, Billy focused his gaze where Adams pointed and joked that he also saw the Woolworth Building floating on the Ross Sea.

Russell Owen recouped in the relative peace of lighter swells and was able to finally file a significant story about how the men saw their first tabular icebergs: "sentinels of ice 20 miles in length and 200 feet height. Drifting north and gradually melting away." These giant ice cubes had calved from the Ross Ice Barrier, and the amazed crews dodged a route through the curious chunks of ice, some tipped up to form odd flat-topped shapes that occasionally glowed blue in the southern light. To put the size of these twenty-mile icebergs in perspective, one scientist on board reminded Billy that Manhattan was only twenty-four miles long.

The expedition's new second in command, geologist Laurence Gould, gave lectures at night, and no good question went unanswered. Why are the cracks in the icebergs blue? The light spectrum, he explained, bounced down into the cracks; the longest wavelengths (red) were absorbed, but shorter wavelengths were refracted back. Gould had much to say about the patterns and textures of ice. And did they know that icebergs, as overwhelming as they were on sight, could be four times larger below the water? Melville and Brown would have to navigate carefully; no one wanted to go the way of the *Titanic*.

Crews worked twelve-hour shifts on the rough sea with ice blockading their path. It was unseasonably cold this year, with more sea ice than anticipated. By December 11, nearly a week after they were due to reach the barrier, they had transferred eighty-seven tons of coal from the *Bolling*'s hold to the *City of New York*; as pretty as the sails looked, the ship ran on a combination of wind and fuel. Malcolm Hanson, the chief radio engineer, told reporters over short-wave radio that the crew would no longer transmit messages except in emergencies, to focus all manpower on the task of survival. "But everybody is well and very busy," he hastened to add.

As each captain slowly made his way through Antarctic pack ice, with the ships occasionally hitched together, crews began to spy regional wildlife, especially whales. "Any pink whales?" Billy often joked to Adams. Animal lover that he was, every whale call had him bolting to the bridge. He learned there were eight species of whales near the pole, and yearned to see a blue, the largest animal on Earth, though there was no denying the others' magnificence. Seeing a whale with its tail in the air set his heart racing, and there were plenty of scientists on board to point out the difference between a minke and a humpback. There was no classroom like the ocean. After days, he finally saw his blue.

Giant grey birds were observed sweeping overhead by the most vigilant birdwatchers on board. One sailor found them rather rat-like. There were seals, too—the Weddell seals spotted on the ice floes wholly unafraid of man. About eight feet in length and weighing a ton, they were named by the early-nineteenth-century English explorer James Weddell. Perhaps if Byrd discovered new species in his flights over the interior, he would give his name to them.

By December 17, another week was gone, and the party was still at sea in ice and winds that slowed progression. But on that day, crew members spotted the first emperor penguins. These four-foot-tall barrels of fat—if you live in Antarctica, it's good to be big-bellied, especially if you want to survive the winter—were first encountered on Captain James Cook's second voyage in the late eighteenth century. For a while after Darwin's evolutionary theories finally caught hold, emperors were thought to be a possible evolutionary "missing link" between birds and reptiles. Scientists believed they could prove this by carefully observing the emperor embryo as it matured. On Robert Falcon Scott's second and last Antarctica expedition, a small side party, including twenty-four-year-old Apsley Cherry-Garrard, set out on a winter sledging journey to scour the ice and collect emperor eggs for this purpose, even though the breed lays only one egg per year. This ill-fated trek in the name of science gave rise to what in Billy's day was considered the greatest of all Antarctic adventure books: Cherry-Garrard's *The Worst Journey in the World: With Scott in Antarctica, 1910–1913.*

The crew spotted the adorable and social Adélie penguins next, discovered in 1840 by scientists on a French expedition led by explorer Jules Dumont d'Urville, who named the penguins and an expanse of Antarctic land after his wife, Adéle. Adélies are ubiquitous along the Antarctic shore. Very short, they have the classic penguin big-belly look, and white rings around their eyes. Many Adélies lay dead on the rocks in stomach-churning decomposition, and dive-bombing seabirds known as skuas came for the feast, gnawing at their open flesh. Billy had never encountered such violence in his library books.

Scientists today identify seventeen distinct species of penguins, but in 1928 there were thought to be only three: emperors, the largest; Adélies, the most common in Antarctica; and kings. The latter are found in more temperate subantarctic regions (outside the Antarctic Circle) such as South Georgia, an island about 1,500 miles east of the tip of South America, and so the men did not get to see them. Each species kept to a strict biological schedule. Emperors were done breeding in November, but Adélies were very busy in December when Byrd's men came across them, building nests, mating, and engaging in humorous courtship rituals such as presenting their prospective lover with a rock. The paired lovers then would stand belly to belly, singing loudly—quite a different sound from the sharp *gakking* heard when disputing territory or being pestered by skuas. Almost all Adélies loved walking in lines; there were no leaders, but most seemed more than willing to follow.

A pervasive tang of pink penguin guano was everywhere: big-barnyard nauseating, like a paddock of cow dung laced with di-gested and decomposed fish. That stink!

As they wended through the ice, Captain Brown called Billy to the bridge with good news: Byrd wanted him to catch some pen-guins. He'd promised to take live birds back to zoos; how many yet to be determined. The commander felt that Billy and Siple were perfect for the job, and it would give the boys something to do with their youthful energy.

Harry Adams was charmed watching Billy plodding along on the ice, writing: "He was good at chasing and catching penguins— and here too he went to extremes—because he selected the largest penguin in sight and the farthest away on the ice . . . [A]fter much labor, he brought the penguin on board, only to have it dive over-board and disappear forever."

Billy became an amateur naturalist, recording various penguin spats and dramas in his journal. He loved imitating the loud calls that pairs made meeting up, and watched as they tobogganed on their bellies on fresh snow and dove for krill, small shrimplike crus-taceans. "They were tame towards humans," he wrote in a letter home, "and a little too easy to catch." He felt sorry for his quarry, though Billy was so good at catching them that he soon almost ex-clusively had the job of penguin tender. Siple distanced himself from the task, seeing where else he could be of assistance, and got in with the dog teams.

After setting out from Dunedin, the *Bolling* doubled back to New Zealand to replenish supplies. (Otherwise the ship might reach the barrier with no coal left for its return.) The *New York* kept on toward the prize. Of course, Billy wanted to be at the Ross Sea with the first to arrive, but what choice did he have? The *Bolling* would get to the barrier eventually, in early 1929. At least he could celebrate Christmas properly in New Zealand and look up some of those lovely girls he'd met at the Dunedin docks.

Paul Siple was by this time well aware of the public's fascination with the stowaway—he'd seen the fawning girls in New Zealand—and he was deeply worried whether his wintering-over spot was secure. While never disparaging Billy, in interviews he chose to pretend the other boy was simply not there. Even the penguin-catching passages in his 1931 memoir, *A Boy Scout with Byrd*, make no mention of his supposed friend tasked with the same job.

The good Boy Scout crafted a rather ingenious plan that would permit him to overwinter: the expedition had promised various zoos barrelfuls of seal and penguin skins in addition to live specimens. Skinning penguins was Laurence Gould's responsibility. Desperate to make himself more than a glorified gofer—a novelty assigned to run after birds—Siple broached the overtaxed Gould with a proposal: Was the second in command aware of his Boy Scouts badge in taxidermy? He'd be eager to assist with the dirty work. Thrilled by the suggestion, and overwhelmed by his new responsibilities following Dick Brophy's demotion, Gould told Siple he would talk to Byrd.

In bold headlines, the Hearst newspaper empire crowed that Wilkins, not Byrd, made the first Antarctica flight, on December 20, 1928. Byrd took comfort in knowing that Wilkins had not actually flown over what he saw as the prize: the South Pole. And while Wilkins took handheld photographs on the flight, one of Byrd's celebrated men, Captain Ashley McKinley, would be the first to use an aerial mapping camera: a Fairchild K-3, the finest of its kind. Like the Boy Scout shrewdly ignoring the stowaway, the *New York Times*, Byrd's official sponsor, made little mention of Wilkins's not-insignificant achievement. This strategy worked, and for the most part, few Americans cared, having bought that flying over the South Pole was the real story.

(Ironically, to find many of the records and medals bestowed upon Wilkins, one must travel to the Byrd archives at Ohio State University. Next to the cavernous rooms that hold the Byrd files is a lonely glass case devoted to his once-formidable rival.)

On Christmas Eve, back in Dunedin, Billy received a Radiogram from his parents. There had been a long letter waiting for him, too, when the *Bolling* pulled into dock, written on his father's new company stationery. Rudy thought it would do his son good to know the family would have no Christmas tree this year without him home to trim it. They had decided to have Christmas dinner at the Polish National Home in Manhattan with their many friends and relatives. "Babcia is not going to be with us," he wrote. "She prefers the quiet at home."

It was a very fatherly message, reminding the boy that his letters home were lifelines for his tearful mother and grandmother, and stressing that no matter if the labor was great or small, the key was to do it well. His performance was his future. Everything in the world would be his if he followed that golden rule.

Billy was surprised to hear he was still a staple in the news, especially in the New York papers. Were his parents really besieged with reporters wanting to hear about the stowaway boy? His father begged him to add humor to his stories so he could share them with the papers and keep his name in Americans' minds. Did his son know that Polish Americans were excited to hear about the Polish flag that Rudy had sent with Billy to take to the ice? He reminded him to have it autographed by all the men.

Rudy was sure to include a report on Billy's beloved bees. He had packed the poor creatures into a box, worried how they would live through the winter, but the little things seemed happy and were making lots of honey: eight to ten pounds this season. He would send some to the Ross Sea! Although the women of the house prayed that Billy would be home soon, Rudy urged his son to do his all to make the wintering-over party, writing, "The farther you go will be a credit to you on return. Don't forget, because there will be lots to learn!" His mother wanted to know if his nails were clean.

Finally, Rudy enclosed a long story about Billy from one of his favorite journals, *Poland* magazine, and mentioned that Babcia was sitting knitting stockings by his side. The father couldn't hide his immigrant's pride about his son turning into an American celebrity.

Moved by the heartfelt updates, Billy had the good sense to write his mother that reading the letter brought him to tears.

The fifty-four-man crew of the *New York* finally arrived at the Ross Sea on Christmas Day. (Having crossed the international date line, the crew marked Christmas twice.) Casting off the *Bolling*'s towline ended the supply ship's responsibilities after having transported the *New York*; the latter was left to fend for itself in the pack ice, crunching through the nearly continuous frozen mass off Victoria Land.

Christmas was a welcome antidote to homesickness. Canadian physicist Frank Davies, known already for his infectious laugh, appeared on deck as Santa Claus in a full red suit that he had packed for the occasion. On ice he would have the less jolly task of taking measurement of the Earth's magnetic field.

The *City of New York*'s triumph made news internationally,

Russell Owen's poignant reports tugging at heartstrings around the globe: for Christmas, Byrd had told Melville to abandon fuel rationing, and they sprinted toward the goal.

KDKA Pittsburgh, the first full-time radio station in the United States, transmitted Yuletide wishes from American-based family to expedition staff. The radio announcer had a surprise for "the nervy stowaway" now back in Dunedin: emotional greetings from his father and mother. "We miss him so much," Rudy told a reporter a few days after the broadcast. "This has been the first holiday season he has been away. But we know he is well cared for and receiving a good education. He will be a man when he returns."

Captain Melville stopped his ship first at Discovery Inlet but spied a more satisfactory landing field with flat, solid ice in a section of the barrier near the Bay of Whales. The *New York* inched closer, sometimes smashing into the sea ice to quicken the advance. When the ship at last pulled up alongside the barrier, crew members anchored her to the astounding cliff that rose from forty to a hundred feet above the water; a sheer wall in parts. The huskies were released from their cramped quarters and went wild with joy.

If only Billy could see what the *New York* crew saw now. Whales smashed tails in the water: blues, a hundred feet long and a hundred tons, bigger than dinosaurs. The foremost consumers of the Ross Sea rose out of the ocean: orcas, better known as killer whales. Russell Owen, there as witness, was beside himself. It was whale soup out there! Finally, he could do true picaresque reporting on the whales' loud sighs and quick gasps of air that fascinated even the most jaded.

The men unloaded the cargo onto the sea ice and used the dog teams to haul it through crevasses and gullies and up a natural ramp they'd discovered onto the barrier. From there they sledged a few miles to the site Byrd had selected for the base camp: Little America. By the first week of 1929, a permanent base had been established.

While Roald Amundsen had built his two miles from the shelf, Byrd moved his crew eight miles inland on the great Ross Ice Barrier.

Teeth clacked in one of the windiest, coldest places on Earth. The furious whips of katabatic winds—caused by frigid air hitting the ice cap and spreading across the continent—were one thing to read about and quite another to experience. What a naïve idea the first-timers had of working in inclement weather: even in the relative warmth of the Antarctic summer, when on a lucky day it would reach 30 degrees, if the famous high winds of the region hit, it could feel well below zero. The men waited until the extremely changeable weather improved to finish unloading the *New York*. (The motorized vehicle pottering along the ice soon broke down; so much for the modern idea to test heavy machinery on ice.)

Still, in a few days, their first iteration of a base camp was beginning to feel homey. Pilot Bernt Balchen shot a seal for dinner, and the cook served everyone dark, chewy seal steak. Malcolm Hanson's radio worked perfectly, picking up programs in several languages, including English from New Zealand and Spanish from South America.

Byrd was ready for his first Antarctica test flight on January 15, exploring 1,200 square miles in a Fairchild aircraft with a single 425-horsepower engine. Marine captain Alton Parker was selected as pilot. Bennie Roth—the hero of Billy's childhood friends; the orphaned Jew born on Avenue A—won a cut of cards and became Antarctica's first sightseeing passenger. Still ignoring Wilkins's achievements, the *Times* wrote that Byrd's test run of his airplane *Stars and Stripes* was the first appearance of a plane over the Antarctic ice. Adolph Ochs, the paper's powerful publisher, felt that minimum mention of Wilkins was the best way to keep his considerable financial investment in Byrd's success worthwhile.

• • •

The *Bolling* left Dunedin on January 14 to join those already at the barrier, but Captain Gustav Brown was quickly instructed to turn around: the sea ice was freezing, even more than before. Impatient, he radioed, "We'd go through hell for you, Commander."

Byrd's reply: "It is warm in hell but thirty-two below zero here, so stay where you are."

The *Eleanor Bolling*, with Billy on it, arrived at last at the Bay of Whales on January 27, the sea ice having thawed sufficiently. The ecstatic crew tied the ship to the *City of New York*'s side. The men were glad to see one another, alliances be damned. Roth, that lucky duck who'd gotten the first glorious aerial views of the continent, showed nothing but kindness for Billy, his fellow rascal from the Lower East Side.

Billy couldn't get over the size of the Ross Ice Barrier, which was more dramatic in person than any journalist could have ever described. Nothing reminds you of the minuteness of your existence like standing at the foot of a mysterious unknown land. The bright sky above him filled in blue, the light mesmerizing. Antarctica was otherworldly, a dream version of a Jack London adventure book— even like being on another planet. Awestruck, Billy struggled to listen as those in command explained the work to be done. He would soon be part of building Little America: the bunkhouses, the mess hall, a machine shop, and an administrative building.

The supply ship was secured as close as possible to the top of the barrier (a portion where it was lowest), and tall ladders were stretched across diagonally for men to climb up to the ice. Unloading the four hundred tons of new cargo was a risky business, all knew, as the barrier ice could calve off at any time. Laurence Gould went over again how to recognize danger: thick ice goes white, so avoid walking where the ice was clear. Even taking a pee in tide cracks (the small cracks caused by tides separating the sea ice and the edges of the barrier) could be hazardous. The two doctors cautioned the men to be careful of all things, even sunstroke in mid-January. This was the warmest part of the Antarctic summer, and with the sun out twenty-four hours, after a full day of manual labor, they might even overheat on ice.

There were twenty-five men dotted across the barrier on one of these first unloading days, handling parts of the Ford plane that Byrd would fly over the pole after the Antarctic winter. *Boosh!* Just as Gould had feared, a square mile of shelf ice broke off, with new cracks forming where men stood. Three floes now floated lazily in different directions, with men on each. The chunks of barrier ice were large enough for the men to keep standing with their cargo, though the aluminum wing of the Ford plane had tumbled partway down a gap in the ice. Fear gripped all near. Lives were at risk, and if they lost the Ford wing, there would be no South Pole flight—the signature event of the two-year endeavor. Of the three planes on the expedition, the powerful Fokker trimotor was the only one suited for such an arduous flight.

Billy, who had been working on the scene, lay down, and while others held his legs, he slipped into the big crack and, dangling, "got hold of the pedestal, and the airplane sections, and pulled them out," reported the *New York Times.* He was ordered out as the rift expanded. Byrd, taking over operations with a megaphone, called for his men to put on life belts.

Billy's young body fat helped prevent hypothermia. Harry Adams pushed him a ladder, and Billy ran to the *Bolling*'s fiery stokehold he knew so well. Shivering but unruffled, he switched into dry clothes and was back in an hour to clean a propeller clogged with ice, gaining new respect from the amazed expedition crew. He hoped that Byrd noticed, too.

The commander did. Bedridden briefly from the cold, Byrd

called Billy to him, telling him how proud he was of his heroic effort.

After the crew recovered from the scare, hard labor resumed. Byrd called the men together to explain that they must all get to work, including him, to move Little America another five miles inland, where the ice was less fragile. The village would be built approximately eight hundred miles from the South Pole, Byrd said, from prefabricated four-inch walls painted orange to be seen easier from the sky. From horizon to horizon, there would be nothing but ice.

The crew worked quickly and dutifully, unloading the remaining cargo in five and a half days. Tottering on the level, snow-dimpled surface of the barrier was much easier then ascending it, and, once on top, they had fairly level traveling to what would soon be the new Little America. Byrd named the route Kit Carson Trail, after the man he had traveled with in the Philippines, who had given him a chance to prove his worth at a young age.

Sledge-loads of stores were connected to the dog teams, and everyone hastened to transport supplies: coal, food, more gasoline, and two extravagant pianos, one of them a player piano. (How much "medical" liquor remained was never mentioned.) Billy helped relocate the two thousand books that would be part of the underground library, complete with fine leatherback chairs. Back in Bayside, he had pasted into his scrapbook a *Scientific American* story that itemized the books that a New York City lawyer named David T. Layman had purchased for the expedition. There were plenty of Sherlock Holmes stories, six Zane Grey Western adventure novels, Jules Verne's *Twenty Thousand Leagues Under the Sea*, and fifty humor books. Layman had also thrown in some goodies for the most erudite, such as Friedrich Nietzsche's *Thus Spake Zarathustra*, George Santayana's *Essays*, and Will Durant's *The Story of Philosophy*.

Foundations were built deep in the snow for the two main

buildings Billy helped construct: Little America's administrative headquarters and the mess hall, which was not large enough for the men to eat in all at once. There would be shifts. It wasn't long before the shacks were covered with snow, with only the stovepipes peeking out. Long tunnels hollowed out of ice were lined with food and instruments and kennels, and connected the two implausibly located buildings built two hundred yards apart. Once completed, it would be unnecessary to go outside. The men chosen to winter over would live like moles under the snow in houses built from highly insulating ceiba tree pods that had traveled from America.

But the heartless cold wearied all. Parked at the Ross Sea, their ships were the southernmost ships on Earth, and now they were constructing the southernmost village in the world. Billy's childhood dreams of getting a real taste of polar misery were a little too realized in the bitter weather of the barrier, as wind whipped up his neck. Pink faced and teeth chattering, he slogged through his daily January assignments in pain, though he dared not tell anyone. Everyone was essential, he told himself, even if he was a mere cog. Byrd would lavish praise on all who deserved it.

Radio operator Carl Petersen had huge news: he had communicated with operators in Spitsbergen, Norway, in the Arctic Circle archipelago up with the polar bears and walruses—modern technology connecting the ends of the Earth. The tired men broke out in applause.

A Radiogram that Petersen sent from Billy provoked similar excitement in the Gawronski household. Rudy and Francesca now had proof that their "ill-disciplined" son had made it to the famous barrier: "Mother. Father. Warm Greetings from a cold country. We are living on the barrier at the Bay of Whales in the most southerly of American villages in the world Little America, Antarctica."

This wasn't quite true. Billy was bunked not in Little America but on the *City of New York*, where he had first stowed away, although he made many trips to the emerging village as ordered. During one excursion up the barrier, he fell in the water, "a sea thick with slush ice and killer whales, and the weather [12 degrees] below zero." He was able to clamber out and warm up again in the flickering light of the stokehold. But he was young; another man might not have fared so well.

Work never ceased, except when blizzards hit, and then even the hardworking dogs curled up in the snow. On the rare break, Billy rested on the ice or his bed, moored alongside the barrier. He ached—but he would not let himself cry. The constant sunlight of Antarctic summer should make it impossible to sleep, but at night the crew was so tired, it didn't matter.

As soon as the weather let up, the man-hauling resumed. Billy's latest assignment was to hunt seals and skin them so that the forty dogs would have meat over the long winter. On off-hours, when he had the energy, he played with the baby Weddell seals and the penguins. He listened to the radio on the *City of New York*, read, played cards and checkers, ate candy, and smoked those free cigarettes donated by Chesterfield, the official cigarette of Little America. It wasn't all that different from the passage through the Pacific, really. If it wasn't so exhausting, it would almost be dull.

Then the drama that Billy had wished for occurred. On January 31 the *Bolling* was getting ready to leave for New Zealand when the ice broke again, stranding several men on floes that began floating away. The ship listed far to starboard and almost capsized. Thirty-six-year-old former US Army Air Corps mechanic Bennie Roth fell into the Ross Sea. Bennie yelled out that he could not swim. How had he never admitted this in his interview? Byrd was distraught, but within seconds, Billy dove into the 28-degree water, perhaps not realizing that in such frigid temperatures, even swimmers could go into shock and die. But in his mind, what was there to fear? He'd gone with the Polish Falcons on so many midwinter river swims.

Now was the time for Russell Owen to bash away at his typewriter. Danger was a great sell, and he wisely (if unjustly) made Byrd the hero of the day: "One's heart stood still for a moment. There was a cry, The Barrier Has Broken! On deck men were calling Commander! Commander!—I'm coming, Bennie, he shouted! Two of his men grabbed Commander Byrd and refused to let him go. 'I can get him, let go, let go,' pleaded Commander Byrd."

Fortunately for the two-man film crew, they had been on the scene and caught some of the all-too-real action. A small rescue boat was lowered and began filling dangerously with seawater. Twenty-four-year-old aerologist Henry Harrison, hanging on fifty feet down the barrier, was saved before he could die of hypothermia, encased in ice.

That night, as all recouped, the pregnant husky Josephine gave birth to six puppies. How could dog lover Billy, dried off and warmed up, not come over for a look?

Two days later, Captain Brown headed back to Dunedin in treacherous weather with a crew of twenty, including Kess, Billy's friend from the Black Gang. Although Billy adored the captain, his heart leapt, for he was not assigned. Perhaps, just perhaps, he was going to overwinter after all.

The Matson freighter *Golden State* arrived in the pretty city of Auckland on New Zealand's North Island on February 11, 1929, with a very familiar mess boy: Bob Lanier. Bob had been relentlessly goaded during the journey; to get his goat, someone even posted on the message board that another "colored boy" had flown over the South Pole. He knew the most racist members of the crew resented his ambition, and that men among them spent the voyage drinking did little to help. But Lanier had made it to New Zealand. True, his plan was vague: to get in front of Byrd and plead for another go. But why should his luck run out now?

Then he was in the news again, but not for reasons he ever wished for: Bob was accused of stabbing a boatswain named John Murphy earlier the same day. Murphy would live, but the court record was grim: "The evidence indicated a wound by a butcher's knife, about three inches from the heart." Bob pleaded innocent: self-defense. Bob's counsel stressed that his client had "lived in terror of his life, and had acted under provocation and constant melees."

Back in the United States, black papers such as the *Indianapolis Recorder* covered the alarming news, but at first they were alone in believing Lanier's innocence. New Zealanders hardly knew what to make of it all. Why would he stab one of his shipmates the day they reached shore? Where was the motive? "Trouble on the ship," a friend of Murphy's would tell the press.

Lanier was allowed to stay out of prison, and earned money for food by making and selling wax paper flowers—a man at the docks had taken pity on him and showed him how. Interest in the young man swelled; this quiet country was used to petty crime, not murder. The *New Zealand Truth* ran a half-page photo of "The Smiling South Pole Boy." Lanier was surprised that public opinion had started to go his way.

On February 18, with twenty-four hours of sunlight, and the aid of his four-member pilot team, Commander Byrd explored forty thousand square miles from the air in one day. He named a low-lying snow-covered mountain range after sponsor John D. Rockefeller Jr.—Laurence Gould, second in command, cracked later that his boss named it after the signature on a $100,000 check. He dedicated a peak to a carpenter on both of his trips, Charles "Chips" Gould (every ship's carpenter was nicknamed "Chips"), and yet another to Billy's original champion, toothless cook George Tennant, which must have tickled Tennant to no end. Later in the year, he would name another range he helped discover after sponsor Edsel Ford. The entire region he labeled Marie Byrd Land, after his ever-loyal wife. Still, Byrd kept to his plan to hold off his more dangerous flight over the South Pole (harsher weather, hours away from help) until after the Antarctic winter, when, with aid of able meteorologists, he could pinpoint the optimum moment for likely success.

Byrd assembled his crew two days later, after going down his list of men as coldly as a chess grand master considering his best move. He was ready to announce which forty-one of the remaining fifty-six had been selected to join him for the winter—or as his men saw it, those he was getting rid of. Some of the discards would kick around New Zealand before being summoned back to ice at winter's end to collect those luckier than them. Others would return to New York.

Almost immediately, Billy learned he was a goner.

He stood to hear the rest of the names in stunned silence. The news was real. The remaining men tried not to gloat, though Paul Siple's wide smile gave away that he'd been tapped for a spot. Byrd allegedly never planned to let Siple winter over because of the potential for PR disaster if the "little Boy Scout," as Siple bitterly referred to himself, lost so much as a hair on his head while under Byrd's care. But Siple's coddling up to Laurence Gould had proved very effective. His selection as the new taxidermist, even more than his initial triumph as the lucky Boy Scout, would lead to his storied career in polar science lasting four more decades.

Lump in his throat, Billy tried to hold on, but reporter Russell Owen was not the only one to spot his tears. More seasoned men were able to hold back cries—there is innate behavior, and there is learned behavior.

The commander took a walk with his youngest crew member, to rally his spirits. His adventures were far from over, Byrd said.

Hadn't he told him his heroic work would be rewarded? Billy would be allowed to come back on the rescue party after winter, and not everyone returning now with him was being asked back. Why, Byrd and Hilton Railey even had another job for him: the public loved the Polish stowaway, and the public relations whiz would set up some interviews in New York. Billy's new assignment was to bring news of his expedition to the waiting public—a stowaway report. How would he like to be on the radio, representing the expedition? Selection, he told Billy, boiled down to who was most useful where. Billy was good copy best used elsewhere. Wasn't he a sworn member of Byrd's Loyalty Club? He was looking for loyalty now, not tears.

News of who had been designated winter-worthy cloaked the brand-new village of Little America with an odd mood, with men trying not to gloat, men trying not to cry.

There were fifteen slated for the *City of New York*'s return from the Bay of Whales—from Adams to Wallis—and they boarded for Dunedin on February 22, given just two days to say their farewells. Billy was now sailing aboard the flagship he had swum to so many months ago, and he would have plunged into the frigid Ross Sea and paddled back toward the barrier if it would have allowed him to stay on ice. He was not just sad; he was scared. He knew from those who had traveled on the *New York* how cruel Captain Melville was said to be; a man who ignored Byrd's egalitarian directives and favored officers, forcing the common crew to keep four hours on, four hours off watch, denying them a good night's sleep.

As Billy battled his disappointment, in a second act of benevolence, Byrd (still spelling Billy's name wrong) sent a follow-up Radiogram from his new Little America radio station, WFBT:

Gavronski: Heartiest congratulations for the part you played in winning the battle through the ice and storms—stop—I was

with you in thought throughout the fight—stop—I know what
you went through—stop—I am proud of you—stop—Best of
Good Wishes, Byrd.

To Byrd's credit, this would be William Gawronski's most treasured possession throughout his life.

The men in Little America settled down to life in what was fast approaching twenty-four-hour darkness. But even in hibernation, there was plenty of work to be done. The executive building held desks, drawing boards, a radio lab, and scientific equipment for the physicists, geologists, and meteorologists tasked with staying put. Nearby were the three radio towers—each seventy-six feet tall—a weather station, and a magnetic observatory. Occasionally, men on the expedition were allowed to communicate with wives and children, but only in an emergency. In their leisure time, bored men made good use of the under-ice gymnasium, which doubled as the only motion picture theater in the world built and operated under the snow. They perused the extensive library of books Billy had helped lug, or listened to the radio or the Victrola, which played records by current musical artists such as Louis Armstrong and Al Jolson. The most popular game was bridge. Byrd, as leader, had his own accommodations (and his own books) in a partitioned section of the library, where his fox terrier named Igloo, a veteran of both ends of the Earth, would sleep at his side. (Igloo wandered the ice in his own snowsuit and boots.) For the rest, there were two bunkhouses, one doubling as a mess hall. To bathe, men had to melt snow and stand in a pail in their bunks, something so uncomfortable to pull off that it was not often done. (Melted snow also provided water for the photo lab.) To snag a snack or a cigarette, they had to venture down a dark tunnel of ice in the newly built "city."

The overwinterers used snow-covered tunnels to roam between

buildings, trenches that Billy had helped excavate. Each structure had to be separated by at least a hundred yards, the size of a football gridiron, to reduce fire hazards. Similar trenches were built to house the weary dogs that had hauled the fuselage of the Ford trimotor aircraft—the *Floyd Bennett*—to an ingeniously constructed igloo hangar before the last glimpse of sun. The working dogs lived in what was dubbed "Dog Town," but puppies born on ice were kept outside until winter came for good, including Ski and Ski, the adorable pack dog who became a favorite of Holland Tunnel engineer John O'Brien; he would bring the dog back to New York City and adopt it after the expedition's end. The chained dogs had little room to move, were fed chopped frozen seal carcasses, and drank from melting snow.

On April 19 the shocking-pink Antarctic sun set and would not be seen for another 125 days.

Billy's old friend George Tennant, a teetotaler, was among the men to winter over, as the cook from the flagship, Sydney Greason, had become a notorious drinker by February. From safe inside the mess hall, Tennant rustled up meals for the hungry, sun-starved men: biscuits and bacon, griddle cakes, oatmeal cakes, ham and eggs, peanut butter sandwiches, soup, chocolate, steaming coffee, and ice cream made from powdered milk, dehydrated eggs, sugar, and melted snow. The barreled beef brought from New Zealand had gone rancid, but luckily there was penguin and that other Antarctic bird, skua, that he had thought ahead to preserve in ice. There was mutton from New Zealand, and very local whale and seal—used in recipes such as whale meatballs and crabeater seal cooked in tomato sauce. Vegetables were another matter. The dehydrated vegetables were inedible, it was later learned, for good reason: they had been dehydrated a decade earlier back in World War I.

Although many days were spent inside, there were memorable

peeks at the aurora australis—the southern lights—glowing midwinter skies of purples and yellow-green.

Russell Owen covered it all in his cable dispatches back to New York:

Thirty-three-year-old Norwegian sea and ski man Christoffer Braathen (who, in winter months, was in charge of the oil hut and thus called the Oil King) passing his 1,500 hours of spare time building a miniature model of the *New York* out of parts carved from wooden engine crates. The model would later go on display at the Biltmore Hotel.

Ice pilot Sverre Strom, the man who first caught Billy aboard the flagship, constructing spare dogsleds.

Into Owen's reports went unusual beard contests and an Antarctic Follies performance featuring "chorus girls" and musicians in blackface, meant to amuse one another and those Americans following along. "Medicinal" alcohol was mixed with lemon powder for a local specialty they called a blowtorch. Byrd even went a little wild himself, dressing—according to aerologist Henry Harrison's one-volume diary, held in the US National Archives—as a "perfect waterfront dollar whore" during a football game in the mess hall. However, Owen apparently considered it beneath mention that Bennie Roth became the first to celebrate the Jewish holiday of Passover on the ice. (Why is this night different from all other nights? Because it's fifty below freezing.)

The men would while away the months, captive beneath the snow, until the return of the sun.

SEVEN

THE STOWAWAY
REPORT

There were girls in Dunedin. But Billy was told by Lieutenant Harry Adams, For godsake, go home for a year and have fun! Visit your worried parents. Do some public relations; a shrewd young man like you should capitalize on your popularity.

Adams would go with him. After eight months away, he would see his wife.

The journey, mercifully, was uneventful—the dozen men just ordinary passengers on the Union Line mail liner the SS *Tahiti*—but the relationships forged on this return trip would be among his closest for years to come, especially his connection with Adams. Still, there was a curious silence during this stretch, with not even a letter to his parents. Perhaps Billy was ashamed.

The twelve explorers returned stateside during the late-April week that a large scenic area in Utah was designated Arches National Monument (expedition geologist Laurence Gould having advocated for this decision earlier in the decade) and a postal worker foiled an assassination attempt on Governor Franklin D. Roosevelt of New York. The men arrived in San Francisco to a still-booming economy now under the presidency of Herbert Hoover, who had replaced fellow Republican "Silent Cal" Coolidge a month prior—in 1929 presidents were still inaugurated on March 4, not January 20. (No one on the expedition voted, this being decades before absentee ballots came into use.) Among the returning, trumpeted the press, was "Bill Gavronski"—still misspelled and to his annoyance identified always as "the stowaway" instead of fireman or even seaman.

But the stowaway's viewpoint was the most interesting angle! For many Americans, Billy's narrative became the first account they heard from a true member of the expedition—not a designated reporter such as Russell Owen or Joe de Ganahl. As soon as he landed, the interviews began, and touched on matters he wouldn't even necessarily know anything about. He had been there, so suddenly he was an expert: "Gavronksi says that Commander Byrd has already accomplished enough scientific work to justify taking the eighty-two men."

Billy's parents scooped him up when he returned by hitchhiking to the East Coast. His mother couldn't stop kissing him; his babcia would not stop holding his hand. Rudy marveled at how tall he had become in his months away—maybe even two inches more a man. He was fatter, too, his father teased, and Billy confessed he had special privileges due to his friend the cook. His voice no longer cracked.

To Billy's amazement, Byrd had made good on his promises: the eighteen-year-old was already widely advertised to appear on WOR Radio, the newly powerful radio station of the New York area, with millions of listeners for highly publicized events—and indeed millions of listeners tuned in to hear him speak on April 24. Harry Adams, Billy's friend and mentor, joined him on the air, and joked with his pal that although higher in rank, he did not get nearly as much publicity as the reformed roustabout.

Billy gave his highly anticipated speech, prepared by Byrd's PR team, at six forty-five in the evening, proclaiming the expedition's (perhaps premature) success. It had been deemed beneficial to present the expedition as idyllically egalitarian. And so Billy spoke of Little America as a utopia, insisting (somewhat fibbing) that in Little America, class distinctions did not exist. It made a great story: college professors passing coal and tugging at ropes with high school dropouts. "This is the one democracy in which each is each other's keeper," Billy promised listeners, "where the comfort of each is the concern of all. The motto of this expedition is one for all, and all for Commander Byrd. The commander is a man to inspire youthful imagination, and the gods of fate have enabled me to serve him."

The exciting broadcast, listed in papers as "The Byrd Expedition," featuring the famous stowaway was immediately followed by "Rutgers University Music Night."

"Byrd 'Boy Stowaway' Lauds Spirit of Men." The radio address, said the *New York Times* in a significant page two feature, was a notable and widely listened to event, followed by a celebratory dinner at the Polish National Home, the *Dom*, at 19 St. Mark's Place. Billy was the guest of honor in a standing-room-only banquet hall filled with the most visible members of New York's Polish American community. The host for the evening: the stowaway's once-infuriated father, who introduced his son with the most extraordinary pleasure. Toastmaster was Austin Clark, the assistant principal of Textile High School. Aged sailmaker John Jacobson, who had first greeted Billy that August day the boy scouted his hiding spot on the *City of New York*, and now very much a friend, knocked the hell out of the audience with outrageous tall tales of penguins lined up in drill and marching to a lead penguin's command, and about chef Tennant's whale steak tasting like the finest dish at Delmonico's restaurant. Sydney Greason, the chief steward, spoke of what a fine lad Billy had become. There were more ready to toast the hometown hero, including Frederick Meinholtz, in charge of the *New York Times*'s radio plant (transmission station) and the wire services coming in from the Antarctic, and Edward Rybicki, president of the Council of Democratic Clubs and a loyal Polish Falcon like Billy's father.

The hero's welcome made being absent from the southern-most village in the world perhaps not as bad as Billy had thought it would be. Especially when the alternative was hibernating under the snow for four months, playing cards and reading *Twenty Thousand Leagues Under the Sea* with taxidermied penguins for company.

But that's not to say it was easy. During Billy's year away, his half sister Stefanie, now twenty-two, had left Poland for Bayside, and there was considerable shock at no longer being an only child. But Stefanie was quickly involved with men and hardly company. Billy visited his friends from school and the old neighborhood, but there was only so much they wanted to hear about his adventures. They had read plenty, they assured him. Old news. Besides, they were in college now: it was May, they had exams. (Was this . . . jealousy? In the years to come, he would learn which stories not to tell in front of friends, many of whom wouldn't learn he was the youngest member of Byrd's expedition until he died.)

The news cycle had moved on, and Billy was no longer needed for interviews. After several weeks of loafing around, he decided he might as well get some paying work before heading back to New Zealand in the fall. He took a subway to the expedition office, now at 2 West Forty-Fifth Street, suite 1508, and asked if he might have a letter of recommendation. Harry Adams, temping as an administrator there (when he wasn't writing up his memoirs), was thrilled to see Billy and wrote the letter himself: "I would select him for any duty in which character, hard work, and intelligent application are required."

Bob Lanier, newly acquitted of attempted assault, left New Zealand on the ocean liner *Niagara* on June 4, arriving in Hawaii two weeks later. (The New Zealand government paid his fare.) Soon he was in Los Angeles, his surreal arrest behind him, Antarctica dreams quashed once again. He made his way north to the Hotel Mars in Oakland, on Seventh and Filbert Streets, and eked out a living making those wax paper flowers he'd sold on the Auckland docks. "Someday I'm going to get back to the South Pole," he told a reporter. "I'd dare anything to see the South Pole and prove that a black man can stand that climate." He continued north by foot, hitchhiking his way through Oregon and Washington and then out of the United States. In Vancouver, Canada, he (rather unbelievably, but this is true) attempted to go back to Antarctica by pleading unsuccessfully with more ship captains. His optimism astounded editors and readers alike. "I don't know just how," he was quoted as saying, "but I'm going to the South Pole this time for sure. I'm still on my way."

To drum up excitement for the Paramount documentary scheduled for release upon Byrd's return in the spring of 1930, a model of Little America opened that summer in New York's ziggurat-shaped Paramount Building, accompanied by pictures of commercial airlines of the future. Billy visited with his family; his father stopped to tell a few people who was there, eliciting gasps. People called out to other visitors: "Come meet the stowaway!" Eager to report back to Byrd that he had bedrock loyalty, Billy stopped to shake hands with the steady stream of visitors. Who better to point out the main buildings, the masts of the radio station, the meteorological observatory? Was he one of the miniature men in the scene? Billy laughed along, a fine ambassador.

Before long, he left the city again. He and Harry Adams had made plans to ship out from Los Angeles the last day of October, time enough to get to Dunedin before the New Year and rescue the overwintering party in the first days of 1930. But with no leads on a promising job that paid—he certainly wasn't going to spend the summer helping with his father's interior decorating business for free—Billy, restless and drifting, shoved off in late July. He would head down south by train, amble through the Southwest, and end up in San Francisco—classic eighteen-year-old stuff—a little jaunt presumably financed by his parents. From there he was sure he could get a lift, hopefully, to Los Angeles. (Anyone who has been a teenager exposed to freedoms away from home and then forced to return might find it hard to criticize Billy too harshly. Staying in Bayside meant living under his father's rules again.)

Nothing major was going on in the world when he first wrote home, except mild concern about falling stock prices. Always the optimist, Billy told his father he was sure the economy would self-correct.

By the end of his gallivanting, disaster was afoot. On October 18, a Friday, Wall Street investors traded sixteen million shares on the New York Stock Exchange in a day—an unprecedented sign of economic anxiety. Panic struck. The following Wednesday, stocks plummeted 6.3 percent. The next day, 11 percent. There was so much active trading that it caused an elongated tickertape delay. Spooked investors wanted out.

Billy's letter to his folks that Friday was endearing: "Oh! Before I forget, I bought an armadillo in El Paso and sent it home. Hope you received it in one piece—Tee Hee!" A self-portrait was included—Billy as a haloed angel—and he joked unconvincingly that everything he experienced in his side trip through the seedy border towns of Mexico was perfectly innocent. But tucked in with the anecdotes and the cartoons was real financial concern. It all was going to turn out okay, right? Then he begged his mother not to write so tiny and promised he would send a letter from Frisco.

Things did not turn out okay. Despite a grand effort by Wall Street leaders to steady the market by investing enormously in steel and other blue-chip stocks—a stopgap tactic—the market nose-dived again the next Monday. Still, who in 1929 would have foreseen the troubled decade to come? Surely the recession would last a few trifling months.

The stock market reeled yet again on Black Tuesday, October 29—closing at 230 after having soared high at 381 less than two months before. Two days later, Billy, in California now, had the gall to ask his folks for money, as he was "ebbtide low." He was wired the funds and rented the cheapest room he could find, which he called a "cootie garage," for fifty cents. He couldn't even afford the YMCA. Billy apologized for his impertinence but explained that he had to obtain a new passport after being told unexpectedly that his sailor's passport was worthless. (He would be traveling as a passenger.) With everything finally sorted out, he got to the ocean liner *Cora* at one thirty, a half hour before departure.

Another letter arrived at the Gawronski home in Bayside, midtrip. Their gadabout son seemed to be having an altogether pleasant journey. The food was pretty good—not excellent, but better than none—and a small swimming pool had been set up on deck as relief from the heat; no arduous coal passing in the broiling stokehold this time. Old seaman that Billy was, he was happy to miss out on the Neptune rituals, writing cheerfully, "God help the landlubbers."

Despite the worsening economy, the mood aboard the ship was festive. Billy was friendly with the other passengers, and there were some old pals from the expedition, too. Harry Adams was still sneaking notes on the funny former stowaway for his book. Another ship, the schooner *Bretagne*, had wrecked off the coast of Oregon, and the French consul arranged for her Tahitian crew to be transferred to the *Cora* for the journey home. In the evenings, the rescued Tahitians took out their guitars and sang and danced. Billy added some Tahitian profanity to his vocabulary and taunted his mother with news of a church service he'd missed for a siesta. "But don't worry mama!" he wrote, "I'll go next Sunday! Pop is always saying put things off to next Sunday."

Like many teenagers bailed out by parents over the years, Billy added a guilty coda: "I really can't express my deepest gratitude for the $." He promised to buy his mother a grass skirt and beads in Papeete in thanks.

As Billy sailed the Pacific, Bill Haines, the trusted forty-one-year-old meteorologist from the US Weather Bureau who had overwintered on ice, finally okayed flying over the South Pole. After four months of darkness, the sun had risen again toward the end of August, spending a little longer in the sky each day. Before long, Laurence Gould shoved off on a two-and-a-half-month, 1,500-mile dogsled expedition into the Queen Maud Mountains to provide ground support and possibly emergency assistance during the coming flight. He and his five companions also took the opportunity to conduct the first geological and glaciological surveys of the region. The layered sandstones they found at the peak of Mount Fridtjof Nansen helped corroborate that Antarctica was linked geologically to the rest of the continents, which had been an issue of contention within the geological community.

By late November, it was light enough for a good, long flight. Haines waited a week for a blizzard to pass before issuing an optimistic forecast: November 29 was the day. The plane for the historic trip would be the *Floyd Bennett*, named after Byrd's all too recently deceased friend, his pilot to the North Pole, whom he had expected to join in his glorious flight over the South.

Bernt Balchen, a Norwegian all of twenty-nine, and a former middleweight boxing champion, did the actual flying. The aircraft was powered by three engines: one Wright Cyclone and two Wright Whirlwinds. Thirty-three-year-old Harold June, a strong chess player with a calm demeanor, served as copilot and radioman, with thirty-two-year-old Ash McKinley from Missouri the lucky aerial surveyor tapped as cameraman. A fine photographer, he served as stand-in for the Paramount documentary filmmakers, who were absolutely not allowed in the aircraft. Byrd was a mere passenger, yet he would get most of the glory.

Russell Owen had real news again, reporting that the cargo on the *Floyd Bennett* included skis, snowshoes, an aerial camera, food prepared by the kitchen staff, the pemmican (their Danish-made stock of survival rations), and gasoline—all in case of an emergency landing so that the four passengers could survive until rescue. Two unlucky spare pilots were staying behind at the base camp, just in case.

The flight from Little America to the South Pole, one that Byrd had waited almost a year for on ice, took less than a day. He was there and back in eighteen hours, forty-one minutes.

The *Floyd Bennett* made a six-mile circuit of the pole, reaching an elevation of 11,500 feet. (To clear the peaks, they had to discard a 250-pound bag of food.) If there was no sign of new species, at least the vista was breathtaking from above, revealing mountains never seen before. A standard compass was of little use so close to magnetic south, which is where a compass would routinely point, as opposed to the entirely separate geographical South Pole, so the team waited as Byrd used a sun compass and his self-invented bubble sextant to calculate their position. (The sextant, which determined the angular distance between objects, allowed the user to obtain an artificial horizon when the actual horizon was not in sight.) Publicists said that navigation, not flying, was Richard Byrd's true skill— ironic given the popular belief that he either fudged or botched the coordinates of his North Pole flight.

When he determined the likely spot of the South Pole, Byrd dropped an American flag weighted with stones taken from Floyd Bennett's grave at Arlington National Cemetery. McKinley filmed as it fluttered toward the ice.

Byrd's name was added at long last to the list of Antarctica firsts, there alongside sealer Captain John Davis, the first to tread on Terra Australis Incognita (a term that dates back to the ancient Egyptian geographer Ptolemy, meaning Unknown Southern Land) in 1821, and Roald Amundsen, first to the pole in 1911. Unlike his flight over the North Pole, the commander had this on film. There would be no naysayers this time.

Then it was back in triumph to Little America, that "clump of huts buried in snow, the only speck of civilization on the Antarctic continent," as Russell Owen put it so beautifully. When word reached America, it was that rare bright news that aroused pride and wonder—a respite from the gloomy economy. Billy's parents listened on the radio. Everywhere, newspapers sold out.

Imagine the laughter in the *New York Times* editorial room the very next day when they decided to publish an angry letter from multimillionaire Wilbur Glenn Voliva, an evangelist priest and radio broadcaster, and a forceful proponent of the flat-earth theory. Voliva—based in Zion, Illinois—proclaimed astronomy, evolution, and high criticism a "trinity of evils." Over at the tony Explorers Club on Manhattan's Upper East Side, the librarian assigned to clipping mentions of recent exploits was amused, too, underlining the last line so not one reader could miss it: "Commander Byrd must know that the sea is a vast outstretched plane ill-fitted to become any part of a globular surface. The truth is, the Earth is a circular plane."

Those on Capitol Hill better appreciated Byrd's feat. A most uncontroversial bill was voted on in Congress on December 21 and signed immediately by President Hoover. Commander Byrd was now Rear Admiral Byrd, a two-star rank just below vice admiral. Americans soon would have it in their heads that Admiral Byrd had been the one to fly the plane over the South Pole. Whatever bitterness Bernt Balchen had over this he kept to himself, for a time.

Left: After a trip to Europe to visit family when he was three, Billy refused to take off his sailing suit. When anyone asked the little boy what he wanted to be when he grew up, his mother answered for him: "He wants to be a sailor." *Right:* Rudy, Francesca, and Billy Gawronski enjoy Coney Island circa 1920. The beach outings were a treat for this Polish immigrant trio seeking escape from the crowded Lower East Side—and a place for Billy to practice swimming to one day become a proud Polish Falcon like his father.

Fourteen-year-old Billy Gawronski was keen to have his rescued stray, Tootsie, compete in a contest organized by the New York Women's League for Animals. What other dog had been trained to ride a horse? Tootsie's triumph was covered in the *New York Daily News* and the *New York Daily Sun*, Billy's first taste of celebrity.

4

Billy kept a scrapbook in which he pasted photos of his hero, Commander Byrd, like this one from the *New York Times*. After her son's departure, Francesca kept up her own clippings.

5

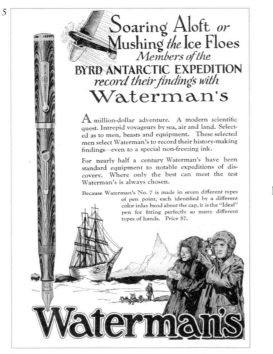

The first American expedition to Antarctica was funded entirely by donations, with no government support. Even the *Times* paid for access, promising no bad press for the Commander. One of many sponsors seeking a share of Byrd's glory was high-end pen company Waterman.

The *City of New York* at full sail. The Antarctica-bound barquentine was an old-fashioned multimasted ship that suggested the previous century—a smart, romantic choice to excite Jazz Age Americans nostalgic for the Heroic Age of Exploration.

Sailors and volunteers packing the supply ship *Eleanor Bolling*. Her cargo included desks, chairs, and typewriters for Byrd's Antarctic office, radios, binoculars, microscopes, coal, donated cans of food, and a black-and-white cat who wandered on board and was quickly named Eleanor by the crew.

Right: Paul Siple whomped his competition vying for the Boy Scout slot with an astounding fifty-nine merit badges, the most of anyone in the nation. The lucky Boy Scout would later become an accomplished polar explorer, authoring four books and coining the term "windchill factor." *Below:* The *City of New York* left Hoboken's Pier 1 with two hundred tons of material and thirty-three people aboard (not including three thrill-thirsty stowaways) shortly before one o'clock on Saturday, August 25, 1928.

Two young soon-to-be rivals side by side on the cover of the *Times*: Paul Siple looking every bit the dutiful son, Billy Gawronski rumpled and disappointed.

Former stowaway Billy Gawronski, now a coalstoker aboard the *Bolling*, is seated front right (wearing a black shirt) in this portrait of the crew. The greenie was subject to his share of joshing his first weeks at sea.

13

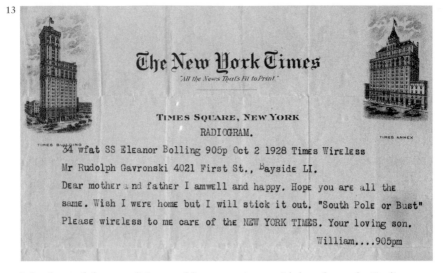

The New York Times

"All the News That's Fit to Print."

TIMES SQUARE, NEW YORK

RADIOGRAM.

34 wfat SS Eleanor Bolling 905p Oct 2 1928 Times Wireless

Mr Rudolph Gavronski 4021 First St., Bayside LI.

Dear mother and father I am well and happy. Hope you are all the same. Wish I were home but I will stick it out. "South Pole or Bust" Please wireless to me care of the NEW YORK TIMES. Your loving son.

William....905pm

Members of the expedition could communicate with loved ones by Radiogram, but anything said was fodder for the press. The public clamored to know more about the plucky stowaway, including if his parents had forgiven him for disobeying them.

14

RADIOGRAM

BYRD ANTARCTIC EXPEDITION

Commander Byrd was notoriously suspicious of those who might speak badly of him, including the *New York Times* reporter along for the journey. This is one of many secret coded messages from Byrd to his publicist, Hilton Railey, back in the expedition's New York City headquarters.

Anchored to the imposing Ross Barrier, the *City of New York* looked like a toy ship.

The expedition may have packed state-of-the-art radios and four newfangled airplanes, but dogs still pulled supply sleds across the ice as they had in the days of Shackleton and Scott.

Billy was part of the team that built the first village on ice: Little America, with its soon-iconic buildings and radio towers. There was also a weather station, a magnetic observatory, and a library with fine leatherback chairs.

After decades of European triumphs in the southernmost continent, Americans thrilled at seeing the Stars and Stripes rising over the ice.

Commander Byrd holding his terrier, Igloo, who, after voyaging to both ends of the Earth, was now one of the most famous and well-traveled dogs in history.

Radio operators successfully attempted the longest-distanced radio signals to date, communicating with a station in Bergen, Norway. They would also keep track of Byrd on his world-inspiring flight over the South Pole.

Finally, the excitement Billy had been waiting for! A sudden break in the ice sent aerologist Henry Harrison tumbling down the side of the Ross Ice Barrier and mechanic Bennie Roth into the frigid Ross Sea. Billy dove into the 28-degree water to help rescue Roth, who couldn't swim.

Left: Some dinners in Little America included whale meatballs or seal steak. There weren't many vegetables, though. Even those dehydrated vegetables that made the voyage south were inedible; it turned out they'd been packaged during World War I. *Right:* Paul Siple had an ingenious plan to convince Laurence Gould to let him overwinter. Was the second-in-command aware of his Boy Scout badge in taxidermy?

Bridge was a popular leisure activity during the four months of hibernation, as were other card games. One man passed his fifteen hundred hours of spare time building a miniature model of the *New York*.

The midwinter Antarctic Follies performance lifted the overwinterers' spirits with acrobatics, chorus girls, and musicians in blackface. Audience members drank "medicinal" alcohol mixed with lemon powder, a local specialty called a blowtorch.

After 125 days of darkness, the sun rose again in late August, and soon the crew could emerge from the ice and dig out the *Floyd Bennett* for Byrd's flight over the South Pole.

Right: Clad in furs against the fierce cold, aerial surveyor Ashley McKinley was entrusted with the Paramount twins' enormous camera to film Byrd's historic flight. No naysayers could grumble that the commander fudged the coordinates this time. *Left:* Byrd's first Antarctic expedition explored an area roughly half the size of the United States, charting ten new mountain ranges—one of which Byrd would name after sponsor John D. Rockefeller Jr.

The people of New York gave a hero's welcome to Admiral Byrd—Commander
no more. The police band struck up "Carry Me Back to Old Virginny" and real
Wall Street tickertape rained down.

Left: Another honor for the Byrd men: dinner in the grand ballroom of the Hotel
Astor. The admiral's portrait may have graced the first page of the menu, but
Russell Owen cheekily proposed that all present raise a glass to Bernt Balchen,
the first to pilot a plane over the South Pole. *Right:* The Paramount documentary *With Byrd at the South Pole* won for Best Cinematography at the third-ever
Academy Awards, although many dismissed the film as mawkish—not that this
stopped Byrdmaniacs from rushing to buy tickets.

32 33

Left: Billy returned from his adventures two inches taller and noticeably more mature. *Right:* Byrd's PR team wrote the kid stowaway's speeches, but Billy would make edits on the page. Vertical lines between words indicate a pause for breath. The onetime "juvenile delinquent" took his public appearances seriously!

34

A reception at the plush Hotel St. George in Brooklyn Heights. In later years, this photo would hang in the former stowaway's living room.

Billy was grateful for work during the Depression, but touring with the American Pacific Whaling Company wasn't one of his prouder moments. Still, that didn't stop Francesca from saving newspaper clippings about her son's travels with the seventy-two-ton whale of San Clemente.

WESTERN UNION

NEWCOMB CARLTON, PRESIDENT   J. C. WILLEVER, FIRST VICE-PRESIDENT

SIGNS
DL = Day Letter
NM = Night Message
NL = Night Letter
LCO = Deferred Cable
NLT = Cable Letter
WLT = Week-End Letter

The filing time as shown in the date line on full-rate telegrams and day letters, and the time of receipt at destination as shown on all messages, is STANDARD TIME.

Received at
12KN R 25XU

FI NEW YORK CITY NY 911AM SEPT 20 1930

ADMIRAL RICHARD E BYRD

DUBLIN NH

DEAR ADMIRAL RECEIVED TWO LETTERS MAY I COME UP TOMORROW MY FUTURE
WORK IN COLLEGE DEPENDS UPON YOU WOULD LIKE PERSONAL INTERVIEW
PLEASE ANSWER SINCERELY

GAVRONSKI

THE QUICKEST, SUREST AND SAFEST WAY TO SEND MONEY IS BY TELEGRAPH OR CABLE

Even Admiral Byrd was having difficulty securing paying work for his men, but getting a kid admitted to Columbia was doable. (Here Billy spells his surname the way the papers did, with a "v" in place of the "w.")

Billy's months shoveling coal in the *Eleanor Bolling*'s dreaded stokehold proved just the start he'd needed for a career at sea. Here he stands on the deck of the SS *Manhattan* in 1937, a third mate in the US Merchant Marines.

In 1943, William Gawronski was given his first command, the SS *Jose Bonifacio*, becoming at thirty-two one of the youngest captains in World War II. He would spend three decades in the Merchant Marines, traveling to every continent but Antarctica.

EIGHT

FINE ENOUGH

The first day of 1930 brought good news for Admiral Byrd. He had feared that the nation's economic woes would wipe out interest in his achievements, despite press guru Hilton Railey's assurances that his triumphant return would have the splashy coverage they all craved. Now Byrd had word that New York's mayor, his old friend Jimmy Walker, had been sworn in for a second term after a landslide November win. At least Walker's reelection ensured a grand reception when the expedition team returned to New York in the spring; Byrd would never be a footnote in history. Billy's parents, struggling to gain new clients and losing most of the ones they had, were relieved, too. They would have something to celebrate, even in these daunting times.

The *City of New York*, like the *Bolling*, had been docked in

Dunedin for the year, receiving paint jobs and repairs but mostly just waiting—not unlike many of her men. On January 6 Billy joined a skeleton crew, including his pal Kess, on the *New York*; they were to pick up those who had nobly wintered on ice. She met a squall right off the bat and soon sent word to Byrd that conditions ahead were dreadful again, the pack ice too severe to break through.

A month later and still not arrived, the *New York* was gifted fifty tons of coal from a whaler fortuitously in the vicinity and began to ram her way through the ice. Hapless crew members chopped a heavy coating of hoarfrost off the rusty ship. Then more bad luck: she was "officially" driven three hundred miles off course by the wind, although there were rumors that Captain Melville had disobeyed Byrd's orders to go straight to Little America and had sailed to within sight of Mount Erebus for a quick look. In any event, the *New York* reached the Bay of Whales on February 18 after forty-four days in combat with pack ice.

As the ship picked its way through what Byrd had renamed Floyd Bennett Bay, Billy's emotions were mixed. Would he be jealous of the epic stories he was sure to hear? Did his secret rival Siple know how popular Billy had become with the press? And yet how could he complain? What others would do to be where he was now!

The overwinterers, with flowing beards (soon to be shaved), had been forewarned that the ice was closing in; they were already at the edge of the barrier, waiting. Weather reports were worrisome; there was one shot to get out. Much was left behind in the rush to sledge to the ship scientific specimens such as soil samples, animal skins, and live Adélie and emperor penguins (kept happy in an iced container). Fortunately, it was plenty light out to load well into the night, and they cast off the next morning at nine thirty, heading the 2,300 rocky nautical miles back to Dunedin.

The men departing had so many tales, and the men picking them up tried to listen without envy. Laurence Gould and his team had scaled a mountain and solved a geological conundrum, Byrd had returned in triumph from the pole. There were inside jokes galore, but Billy was careful not to appear bitter. He had been invited back, after all.

The *New York* had better luck breaking through the galling Ross Sea pack ice on the return trip. Before long, she met up with the *Kosmos*, an immense Norwegian whaler with an impressive hospital on board, whose doctors gladly took on twenty-seven-year-old junior radio operator Howard Mason, stricken with appendicitis for almost a week. The cooped-up dogs and penguins were also transferred to the faster ship, a crate of puppies falling between the two. The crate was fished out, and the miserable puppies dried out over the engine room hatch.

The *New York* arrived in Dunedin two weeks later to an ego-gratifying reception. A band played George Frederic Handel's "Hail, the Conquering Hero" for the "lucky" wintering-over party, which had been away for one year and fourteen weeks. Mostly the Dune-diners were being polite—they had seen dozens of expeditions leave and arrive—but the locals had become quite fond of the Americans. Mayor Robert Sheriff Black escorted Byrd, the man of the hour, to his complimentary stay in the city's finest hotel. Despite a wool-gathering convention that booked up almost every room, beds were found for the remaining expedition members in private homes. The lesser-known seamen scrambled to make themselves presentable for the pretty ladies of the house; girls, not glory, dominated their minds.

Howard Mason, his appendix removed, joined the revelries. Byrd had not lost a single man in the Antarctic, an incredible feat.

Many of the men had trouble adjusting to life in the big (or little) city after a solitary year on ice. Noises overwhelmed, and some were enticed by now readily available alcohol and women. Yet all the Down Under ballyhoo was still (hopefully) only a taste of what was to come back in the States. Although there were dozens of letters from families detailing the bleak economic plight back home, America's troubles were easily forgotten. Every member of the crew knew that Mayor Jimmy Walker's reelection pretty much ensured a big to-do. How bad could things be if Walker planned to shell out for a parade?

Filmmakers Joseph T. Rucker and Willard Van der Veer (now nicknamed "the Paramount twins") set off posthaste for the Americas. There was a movie to be made. They arrived in Cristóbal on the steamer *Tamaroa* at eight in the morning on the last day of March after a monthlong voyage. There the film reels were transferred to a Lockheed Vega Wasp-engine-powered plane helmed by a twenty-nine-year-old named Leland "Lee" Shoenhair, chief pilot for the Goodrich Rubber Company. Shoenhair had set several aviation records already, and now he flew *Miss Silvertown* at record speed over jungles and a volcanic mountain range—making minimum refueling stops and flying at night. The priceless film arrived in New Jersey a mere three days later, a feat newsworthy in itself. Then the celluloid strips received a motorcycle escort to the Times Wide World Studios in Midtown Manhattan, resting in the backseat of a limousine as the car made its way through the Hudson River vehicular tunnel (the official name for the Holland Tunnel). The film could now be out in theaters in time for the expedition's June arrival, maximizing the financial return.

Qu'elle surprise! Captain Brown found another stowaway just as the *Bolling* left Dunedin, a young man named Colin Gillespie, who was later put off in Tahiti. The expedition members barely looked up now when a stowaway was found. It was funny, though: Billy and the other stowaways had been desperately trying to leave New York, whereas this one was presumably desperately trying to make it there. Wherever you're from, there's always somewhere more exciting.

New York had not forgotten Billy. Now that the men were coming back heroes, there was renewed interest in the city's finest. The *Brooklyn Daily Eagle* checked in with Mr. Rudolf Gawronski to see how his son was faring and found that the proud father was certainly enjoying himself. "I got a thrill last Saturday," Rudy told the press, "by going to Schenectady" in upstate New York "and speaking in Polish over the shortwave of WGY directly to my boy."

Back on the *Bolling*, Billy received a telegram from his mother reminding him, "Don't forget to acknowledge Roosevelt's courtesy!" Harry Adams telegrammed back, "*He will do so*." Franklin D. Roosevelt was a great admirer of Byrd, as well as an intimate friend, and had championed adventurous youth throughout his career. Whatever Governor Roosevelt wrote or did for the spunkiest young man in New York remains unknown; most likely he sent his best wishes to the brave boy from his state.

Word trickled back to the men on the ships that New York had some extravagant plans to celebrate their return—not just the traditional parade. Coney Island's amusement park was building a 350-by 50-foot-high cyclorama of Little America, a circular 360-degree painted canvas scene, viewed from inside, complete with astounding animated effects including moving icebergs, penguins, whales, dog teams—even miniature versions of the men working the ice. (The price tag? A staggering $25,000 Depression-era dollars.) Not a small number of the explorers, Billy included, had seen Luna Park's previous cyclorama—depicting the brutal Battle of Château-Thierry, France, which turned the tide of World War I against Germany—a small wonder of New York City with all sorts of electrical wizardry and jets of steam. That spectacle was getting the boot for the likes of them?

As the ships retraced their steps near the equator, the crew—and the dogs—felt the heat. Moose-Moss-Mouse—named by bored expeditioners back in Little America who thought the one-eyed, eighty-five-pound husky looked a bit like a moose, a bit like a mouse, and oddly mossy—tried to break into the icebox with the animal specimens headed to the American Museum of Natural History. There were no live penguins on board; they had been transferred to the whalers long ago. Alas, none of the penguins slated for American zoos would make it to New York alive; they reportedly died from drinking cleaning fluid while being transported back. There's no record if the *City of New York*'s unskinned dead birds were taxidermied on ship, but Siple certainly had time to kill.

Meanwhile in Washington, the US House of Representatives—following a vote to suspend rail mergers until the following March, and another abolishing dial telephones in the Senate wing of the Capitol—passed a resolution awarding medals to all members of the expedition. The wintering-over party received gold, although Byrd alone earned a genuine gold medal; the other "gold" recipients were given medals made of ten-karat gold plated over copper alloy. William Gavronksi, his name misspelled as always, received silver, due in part to his bravery in saving the plane parts and Bennie Roth. Billy was pleased to hear the official breakdown; at least he wasn't getting lowly bronze, as several seamen did. Not bad for a stowaway.

The search was on for the perfect designer to cast the Byrd Antarctic Expedition Medal, although reporters noted it was unusual in a time of crisis for public funds to be spent commemorating an expedition that had received no government money. Not everybody approved, with one cheeky columnist even wagging, "Members of the Antarctic expedition will get congressional medals for proving that a penguin is a bird." Few dared mock Byrd's noble return.

Even inopportune use of federal funds could not dampen the

public's enthusiasm for the heroes' return. On May 31 more than five thousand Polish schoolchildren marched from Billy's childhood church of St. Stanislaus on East Seventh Street to city hall to celebrate the sensational stowaway. Their spirited march made national news.

As the *Bolling* and the *New York* approached New York City, the ships slowed to travel together and weigh anchor side by side. It would make for better photos.

The flagship pushed through the mist just after two in the morning on Thursday, June 19, with Admiral Byrd above deck in his signature khaki, holding the instantly recognizable terrier Igloo, who was now one of the most traveled dogs in history. Waters were so choppy that although Byrd's wife, Marie, had specially chartered a tug to greet her husband, Byrd could only wave to her instead of joining her for a true reunion.

Passports were checked and both ships cleared by the Scotland Lightship Quarantine Station out in Ambrose Channel off Sandy Hook, a formality rather than the rigmarole that immigrants entering the United States through Ellis Island were put through; bona fide seamen could be inspected quickly on deck per the Immigration Act of 1924. Black-and-white cat Eleanor was likewise waved through. "Fit to lick any dog on ice," as the *New York Herald Tribune* put it, she had made a remarkable two-year journey on the *Eleanor Bolling*.

Six marines from the Brooklyn Navy Yard arrived with valises full of fresh uniforms, so that the men of the hour could come to shore spic-and-span. Rear Admiral Byrd changed into his white duck uniform, the black shoulder straps and gold epaulets reflecting his newly improved status.

Long before dawn, crowds massed at Battery Park's Pier A at the southern tip of Manhattan, with more than five thousand people

(Billy's parents among them) there by ten o'clock. The roofs of buildings near the pier were filled, and the Battery Park elevated rail was so chock-full with onlookers that it risked collapsing; police made the crowds descend. A detachment of 400 sailors and marines was sent from the Brooklyn Navy Yard to help preserve calm, joining 2,400 policemen on foot and horseback. Officers locked arms in a human chain to control pushing crowds.

What had these thousands of people come out to celebrate? To a certain extent, public excitement about the returning heroes stemmed less from their achievements, which were too scientific and technical for many to understand, than from the spectacle of it all. But perhaps those wags in the media who scoffed at the expedition's smallish contributions to science missed the point. The expedition may not have found lost dinosaurs or calculated just how many frozen miles the southernmost continent spanned, but wasn't making Americans aware of Antarctica not enough of a legacy? Now so proud of their Antarctic adventurers, like the Brits, the Norwegians, and the Belgians, the American people truly considered exploration of the icy continent part of their own heritage and would for years to come. The United States would now dominate scientific research on Antarctica as well, much to the chagrin of the Europeans.

The first three boatloads of official welcomers—including New York's well-paid chairman of the Mayor's Committee on Receptions to Distinguished Guests, Grover Whalen—set off to greet the admiral midmorning. Marie Byrd, fed up with the chaos already, stayed onshore, but Eleanor Bolling Byrd made sure that *she* was on board the official cutter picking up her son. ("Greeted by Mother: Wife Not on Tug" was one of several wire service subheadlines that could not have gone down well.) Mrs. Bolling Byrd gave the day's first recorded greeting, asking loudly, "Where's my child?" and adding, "The next time you start on an expedition someone ought to chloroform you!" The mighty Byrd tribe (minus the good wife) had ten minutes of private reunion, with Dickie's brother Harry, the now-former governor of Virginia, also present for welcoming duty.

In the gentle haze of what would become a hot, muggy summer day, the official tug of the city, the *Macom*, set off with the navy's newest rear admiral on board, while the men who served him followed on the steamers the *Manhattan* and the *Riverside*—even those who had taken part only in earlier stages of the expedition. The New York City Police Department Band blared on the *Macom*, and the Fire Department Band held sway on the *Riverside*, with pushy reporters divided throughout. A flotilla of both official and citizen boats—seventy-seven of them—lined up behind. A dozen fireboats sent thin white sprays of streaming water into the air, and boats docked in Manhattan sold $1 tickets for a ride out to join the maritime parade.

Even the armed forces paid homage to Byrd's gallant civilians: as the fantastic flotilla made its way to New York Harbor, a thirteen-gun salute sounded from Governors Island, home to the Coast Guard. Ships on the Hudson echoed in whistle salute. The enormous navy dirigible *Los Angeles* and two smaller British airships—there for a showing of international respect—passed overhead. One correspondent likened them to "a great whale and her two babies." Other airplanes swooped through the skies.

Meanwhile, without fanfare, the *City of New York* and the *Bolling* headed upriver to dock. In a few days, they would become tourist attractions on the Hudson, with money earned from admission earmarked to pay off the expedition's many bills.

Onshore, the crowd—squished ten deep from the Battery to city hall—was estimated at a half million people, with proud Virginians having traveled up by train or boat to join New Yorkers in greeting their native son. There had been slight changes in fashion since Byrd left two years before. Less expensive fabrics such as cotton jerseys were coming into vogue, and there were notably fewer hats on ladies' heads. Byrd was grateful to hear that the crowd was estimated to be much larger than that for his 1927 parade as runner-up to Charles Lindbergh for the Orteig Prize—though a half million people was still half the number that came out to cheer Lindbergh.

An up-to-the-minute "radio telephone" had been installed in the *Macom*, and Byrd broadcast his first greeting to the nation, complete with "word pictures" of his adventures. Oh, he had had adventures! Asked skeptically about the value to mankind of proving that south polar flight was feasible, a surprised Byrd countered, "Who knows? It was a hundred years or more before our own country was put to use after its discovery."

The police band struck up "Carry Me Back to Old Virginny." This distressed Byrd's terrier Igloo, who howled at the boat whistles and the general cacophony. Perhaps, like some of the men from the expedition, Igloo was having trouble adjusting to all the hubbub after two years of tranquility on ice.

After a forecast of fine weather, it now threatened rain. At eleven thirty in the morning, a truck carrying a thousand umbrellas—a gift from a New York manufacturer looking for press—drove up to city hall, where five thousand city officials had been invited to witness the formal ceremony. Three umbrellas were given to the Misses Roon, Katherine, Mary, and Ann, maiden aunts of Mayor Jimmy Walker, who had arrived sensibly early and had already been shown to seats in the exclusive mayor's box in the spectator stands. The well-loved Street Cleaning Department Band kept the growing crowd amused until the explorers arrived.

Farther south in the city, Byrd's third tickertape parade had begun. The "pride of Richmond and glory of Virginia," the thirty-two-member Richmond Light Infantry Blues, an all-black band in white duck trousers, launched into marching tunes at full blast, followed by the New York National Guard's Seventy-First Regiment in full dress, and Richmond's Sixteenth Infantry Battalion Band in its khakis. A paper snowstorm once again hit the Canyon of Heroes, the grey sky bleached with real Wall Street ticker, torn telephone directories, and adding-machine tape thrown through windows above. Billy rode in one of the cars of honor as the parade proceeded down lower Broadway.

Camera bulbs flashed before city hall at an honest moment of reunion between husband and prim wife, and a father greeting his long-neglected son and pigtailed daughters. Dickie, Evelyn, and Catherine danced with excitement. Daddy was home. (No mention was made of the whereabouts of the Byrds' three-year-old daughter, Helen.)

World-famous soprano Anna Case sang "The Star-Spangled Banner." Inventor Thomas Alva Edison had once used her atmospheric voice to see if people could tell the difference between recorded sound and the live thing.

As Billy and the other men were ushered into reserved seats, the man of the hour was welcomed onto the columned rear portico of city hall by official city welcomer Grover Whalen, who said to Byrd, somewhat unthinkingly, "You have here as magnificent a reception as Colonel Lindbergh received." The praise for his rival smarted, and both knew it was not really true. As much attention as was being paid, nothing could ever top Lindbergh's flabbergasting reception in 1927. Nothing ever will.

Whalen then called a "birthday boy" to the stage: forty-nine-year-old Mayor Walker, who hailed Byrd as "a great scientist and a still greater human being." Chancellor Elmer Ellsworth Brown of New York University bestowed an honorary doctorate of engineering on the man, and each member of the expedition received the city's Medal of Valor.

Then it was over. Crowds dispersed. A sixty-nine-year-old man attached to the Richmond Light Infantry Blues lay down on a bench and drifted into sleep after having marched in the heat. It took 478 men to sweep up seventy-five truckloads of torn paper, at a cost of $21,915. The parade had been gigantic and gaudy, and the next morning the *New York Sun*, more reliable than the paper of record (it wasn't sponsoring the expedition), declared halfheartedly that it had been "fine enough." It would have been impossible to live up to the hype.

But the festivities were nowhere near through. A grand luncheon was scheduled for two o'clock at the Advertising Club of New York at 23 Park Avenue. Byrd, still in his rear admiral uniform, rode with Mayor Walker in a Ford Model T limousine; the Ford Motor Company was an expedition sponsor, after all. Prisoners in the grey municipal jail on Centre Street, called the Tombs, waved as Byrd passed by, cheering from their cell windows when he waved back. The man who did the actual flying over the South Pole, Bernt Balchen, followed angrily in the car behind.

At the fancy afternoon meal, the exhausted rear admiral was given the highest medal from the American Geographical Society: the David Livingstone Gold. Not mentioned in the *Times* coverage the following day was that Charles Murphy, the club's president, was Byrd's favorite and best-paid ghostwriter.

Most of the Byrd party had not been invited to the event and were instead taken to the Biltmore to collect their accumulated mail, secretly grateful for even the briefest rest. New Yorkers like Billy could now spend a little time with their loved ones or catch a few hours' sleep. Out-of-towners without funds or families crashed at the Seamen's Church's two New York hotels, home to scores of sailors without a ship. Seamen's was (and still is) an Episcopalian-affiliated, partially charitable society that had already worked closely with Byrd by providing ditty bags and first aid kits filled with sewing tools and other useful supplies when his ships left New York Harbor in 1928. Now fifteen of Byrd's party required room and board—not an easy ask, as the lodging houses were already full of mariners seeking refuge in increasingly hard times. The $1 rooms were given to expedition crew members for a heavily negotiated 75 cents, with each man accorded an allowance of $1.50 per day for meals until the celebrations ceased.

Billy, at this point, at least, did not need extra aid, although he had been handed exactly $100 for two years of work upon his official discharge. His parents found him after the parade; his beloved babcia pinched his cheeks once more and held him close.

Then it was back to the draining life of the publicly exalted. That evening, he was expected to attend his first formal dinner (of many) in the grand ballroom of the Hotel Astor in Times Square, an even bigger bash than the luncheon he'd missed, broadcast live by radio stations WOR, WABC, and WNBC. In a dinner coat borrowed from his father, Billy took his place—mercifully, Byrd's expedition heroes were grouped together—at table A, seat 5. The lavish menu was a bounty of food the likes of which had not be seen in the iciest of continents, and would have been scandalous to serve even a year later as the economy fared ever worse.

Coupe of Melon Granada

* * *

Petite Marmite Mikado

* * *

*Celery * Salted Nuts * Olives*
Brook Troute Sauté Almandine with Cucumbers Grenobloise

* * *

Contre-Filet of Beef Chasseur
Fresh mushrooms Forestiere
Vegetables Bouquetiere
Poitrine of Capon in Jelly Nigey with
Bouquet of Asparagus Riviera

* * *

Bombe Ambassadrice
Petits Fours
Friandises

* * *

Moka

* * *

Cigars
Cigarettes
Mineral Water

The "best" families of Virginia graced the room of a thousand, as well as a Who's Who of New York. The hotel band played "Old Virginny" again (a tune everyone was getting damn sick of already, especially Byrd). Prohibition would not end for another three years, so a toast of ice water was made. Russell Owen, who secretly hated Byrd for trying to rewrite his *Times* copy, cheekily proposed raising a glass to Balchen. Byrd smiled big, maybe for show. The camaraderie was outwardly exquisite.

"There's been a sixth successive reduction of bank rate from 3 cents to 2 1/2 percent." The following day's *New York Sun* tucked this worrisome economic news into the same page as its report on Byrd's welcome. A few pages later, another ominous tidbit: the Ford Motor Company, a sponsor of the expedition, would close two plants in Detroit beginning July 12 until further notice, to force employees to take their vacations simultaneously. That same day, a thirty-seven-year-old Wall Street broker named Walter Werner shot himself under the heart, blaming financial difficulties.

Byrd had time for only a brief kip after the reception. The Biltmore Hotel rose to the occasion, running an ad that the hero was asleep in his semipermanent home. "In Little America, they named their most comfortable shack the Biltmore," the ad claimed. All the expedition sponsors wanted a piece of Byrd in his moment of glory. At least in the Antarctic, he had been away from this madness.

As for Billy, following a few hours in his second-story bedroom in Bayside, the nineteen-year-old had to pack again. All the expedition men were to board a midnight train out of Grand Central, arriving at eight thirty the next morning in Washington, DC. If they were annoyed to be put on the road so soon after having been reunited with their families, no one was going to miss a chance to be photographed with the president.

The "Byrd Men" faced another swarm of well-wishers at the capital's Union Station. After shaking many hands, they trailed Byrd single file, waiting respectfully as their leader entered a White House limousine. Once he was off, they clambered onto three presidentially chartered busses headed to the stately Willard Hotel at 1401-09 Pennsylvania Avenue—just two blocks from the White House—where, by special request, the busloads of adventurers could get some actual rest.

Billy nearly pinched himself at the White House later that day. He had been there before—on a group tour in high school with Textile's history club—but here he was among the guests of honor; a hero photographed with a sitting commander in chief. The group photo with President Herbert Hoover on the White House lawn would appear twice that week in the *New York Times*, in the daily edition and the weekend magazine. Billy was now a living legend—at least at his alma mater, where his former history club advisor, Mr. Fliegel, hung up the photo and invited him to address the entire school. He would do so, twice.

The expedition's demanding Washington itinerary included a luncheon given by the National Geographic Society's board of trustees and a tagalong with Byrd to Arlington Cemetery, where Billy watched silently as Byrd placed wreaths on the graves of Admiral Charles Wilkes, the first American to explore the Antarctic; Admiral Robert Peary, reportedly first to the geographic North Pole; and the desperately missed Floyd Bennett. Then they were off to a private screening of the Paramount twins' documentary. Billy was startled to find that not every member of the expedition was listed in the program; the names of those who had in some way angered Byrd were simply not there. Thankfully, Billy's loyalty had secured his inclusion.

The American heroes were not, however, awarded their Congressional Medals that day—a shame, as Billy had hoped to bring his home to his mother; a small token of thanks for forgiving him for stowing away. The medal was finally mailed his way an inexplicable fifteen months later, along with a heartfelt message from Byrd: "This is knighthood that your grateful countrymen have conferred upon you—the highest honor within their gift. This is a recognition that will carry your name on the pages of history."

After a relentless, sledgehammering ad campaign, *With Byrd at the South Pole* opened June 20 at the Rialto Theatre on the corner of Broadway and Forty-Second Street. Naturally there was a rave review from the *New York Times*. "It's a great picture," declared Mordaunt "Freddy" Hall, the *Times*'s first regularly assigned film critic, "one that captures the eye from beginning to end, with a gripping climax." The paper even ran an article by the two filmmakers on how they braved the elements at the bottom of the world.

Less expected praise came from Byrd's most dogged critics, the cynics at the *New Yorker*, who lauded the Paramount twins' cinematography but couldn't resist gibing the expedition's hero worship even when delivering compliments. Their own first regularly assigned film critic, John Chapin Mosher, wisecracked, "It must be noted of [Byrd] that never once in the course of the chronicle of his adventures does his expression for a moment alter."

The British had long prized their significance in the history of Antarctic exploration, and perhaps this explains why their critics bordered on cruel when they reviewed the film in July. One typically jeering review ran in the *London Times*:

> It is hard to believe that the South Pole can be vulgarized, but this has now been done and been done thoroughly. One would have supposed that the Antarctic plateau would have rejected the atmosphere of the studios; but Paramount has marvelously subdued it— split polysyllabic heroics over it, decorated it with sentimental ribbons, trodden it with captions, tickled it with humor, has supplied it with brass bands and flags and letters from home and photographs of the explorers' children on the croquet lawns of Massachusetts—with everything except, by some unaccountable omission, "love interest"—has in brief, found it snow and left it slush.

Time magazine reported the ruffled reactions from across the pond with a bit of glee, and with a wink to readers as to how unsporting the Brits were. Jealous, even.

Still, the British did have a point: the documentary was mawkish. A song from the film that was (wrongly) expected to be a hit—by familiar Tin Pan Alley songwriting duo Irving Kahal and Sammy Fain, best known for the schmaltzy "You Brought a New Kind of Love to Me" and "Let a Smile be Your Umbrella"—included not-so-memorable lyrics such as these: "If pride can build a hero's throne, the world is proud of you alone," and "Like ships that brave a stormy wave, thru Virginia skies you've flown / The Voice of Fame shall sing your name in every dreamer's poem."

Conceived in a time of economic flush, the ambitious picture was released to a Depression-era audience for the price of ten cents or a quarter, depending on the seats. Paramount had so very much riding on the film—not least of which being pride—that *With Byrd at the South Pole* had continuous performances from eight thirty in the morning on; advertisements proclaimed the film "Superbly human with rare humor that only high daring could evoke!" But months of media bombardment had dulled national interest in Byrd and his expensive expedition, and while more than sixty million Americans still frequented the pictures, with the onset of hard times, they itched for stories closer to home. The more popular films during this era, even the comedies, were grounded in classlessness and social realism. (The Byrd documentary's competition in cinemas was the romantic comedy *True to the Navy*, starring "It" girl Clara Bow as a lunch-counter girl who falls in love with a rough-and-tumble sailor.) While the film did not tank—there would always be Billy Gawronski types eager to support their idol in his every endeavor—box-office receipts were respectable but hardly exceptional.

The mostly silent film would nonetheless go on to win Joseph Rucker and Willard Van der Veer each an Academy Award for Best Cinematography, the first—and, to date, only—documentary so honored. Today the movie can be watched in its entirety on YouTube. Billy the stowaway does not officially appear by name, but he can be seen for brief seconds unloading supplies on ice and building an igloo.

•   •   •

Billy, back home in Bayside—dependent on his father for pocket cash, probably getting yelled at by his folks for leaving his room a mess—was almost a normal young man again. But every once in a while, he'd need a lift from his pop to be a guest of honor somewhere posh. The man on the street may have been starting to tire of the heroes, but formal dinners didn't stop: one evening, a bash in the plush Hotel St. George in Brooklyn Heights; the next, a reception hosted by the Polish Democratic Club.

If there were an excessive number of events for Billy to attend, imagine Richard Byrd's migraine: bogged down in luncheon after luncheon, one that served ice cream in the shape of South Pole penguins; another where he was introduced by a ventriloquist's dummy.

At least the social engagements filled the men's days. The Great Depression was still at its start; 1930 was several years away from the three major Dust Bowl storms that would devastate the agricultural heartland. Yet many of Byrd's men struggled to find work. The academics fared best, with most returning to university life; but for the regular crew, any paying job was considered a gift, from line chef to janitor. The shame of unemployment was too much for these men who had been household names. When they left for Antarctica in 1928, only 4 percent of the nation were out of work; now the number was almost 9 percent. One year more, and unemployment would reach double digits.

Not even a month after the expedition's return, the Associated Press ran a story on aerial photographer Ash McKinley's new deployment: to aid the noble volunteers desperately seeking work after demobilization. The kindly Captain Gustav Brown—still living downtown at the Seamen's Institute, where Billy and other favorites would visit sometimes—let newspapers know he was looking to join a whaling mission. Several expedition members, including Billy, were

said to want to get into the "flying game." Even the world's most
famous Boy Scout, Paul Siple, was having trouble finding a part-time
job to pay his way through three more years of college. (To save expenses, he would finish his degree in two.)

As the expedition's remaining salaried administrative staff
searched for paying work for the most loyal, the panicky men, happy
to return favors, were positioned across the country to lecture at
events where the documentary would be screened. (Byrd let his men
know how pleased he was that they were promoting the film without salary.) McKinley helped Billy secure at least five such speaking
engagements in July, including, on the last day of the month, a noon
luncheon at the Oswego Kiwanis club upstate. Most of his lectures
were arranged where he could travel by train in a few hours and at
little expense.

"Antarctica was desolate and forbearing," he told one group of
grown men, "the loneliest of continents, and the absence of a woman's touch is particularly noted in the region about the South Pole."
Fortunately, his religious parents were not in the room to hear that
reveal. Reporters on the Byrd beat (which was getting less prestigious by the day) thought "the boy stowaway" did a splendid—and,
above all, entertaining—job, his speeches filled with tantalizing tid-
bits about why the juices of the whale's stomach were used in the
finest perfumes, and how man-eating sharks would start by ripping
out a person's tongue, apparently "a great delicacy." At least once, he
was followed onstage by a barbershop quartet of singing whalers,
young and old.

After Billy's fine press, Ash McKinley soon had good news: he'd
secured the kid an unusual temporary position as assistant lecturer
and usher traveling the Northeast by railroad car with the American
Pacific Whaling Company, the only American whalers still actively in
business, based out of San Clemente, California. What the position

of "whale usher" entailed was a long story, but Billy, desperate for money, stopped McKinley cold and accepted without asking how much the job paid. (Which was not much: on par with menial labor.)

Good things come in pairs. Admiral Byrd took time out of his wearying fund-raising and bill paying—the expedition was still $100,000 short—to check in on his former stowaway, asking how the kid was getting on. He should write if he needed anything. Billy mulled over what Byrd could do for him; he was sure he could think of something. For the moment, though, he was gainfully employed.

The ads in the papers were enticing:

> Have you seen the whale? The famous whale of San
> Clemente in its own railroad car?
> *Bring the Children!*
> "Not a Stuffed Dummy!"
> "Actual in the flesh!"
> "A Sight of a Lifetime"

When Billy reported for work, whale master William M. Roddy explained that he'd hired him to show off a "monster" fifty-six-foot-long, seventy-two-ton whale being hauled around the United States in a glass-and-steel railroad car. The finback had been harpooned six months earlier off William J. Wrigley's Catalina Island. When not on display, its parts were contained in thirty-eight barrels of embalming fluid so that it could be transported easily. Now in the Northeast, the traveling show had added the Antarctic stowaway as an extra thrill.

> "Worth Coming Miles to Witness": Hear "Gavronski"
> Byrd Lecturer
> Hurry! Note Sensible Admission Prices. Adults 25
> cents, Children 10 c. Hurry!

Billy was slightly ashamed at first of the downgrade from the Byrd expedition but found he enjoyed working alongside veteran whale master Captain Sherman Gaule and a good-natured old salt named "Barnacle" Bill Garrett. But papers wanted to interview only the kid. At least a dozen articles appeared in the Northeast touting the newest member of the traveling sea specimen show. Not that his fellow whale handlers minded: the boy was good for business, and they all were getting paid in hard times.

Over the next few weeks, as the railroad car crisscrossed the Northeast, Billy added intriguing details about the dangerous sea leopards infesting the icy waters of the Ross Sea. He told audiences how the sailors liked to get in the rigging and fire bullets into the pods of "vicious" orca whales. Why, yes, he'd whipped off a shot or two himself. One Connecticut journalist assigned to his story was flabbergasted by the knowledge that the former "juvenile delinquent" had gleaned.

In later years, Billy would write to a friend in Poland that he had come to be ashamed of the grislier parts of his speeches that summer—killing as titillation. He was grateful, reflecting back, that he usually closed his lecture with a warning to the public that the indiscriminate killing of whales would lead to their extinction.

Trading on an all-time-high interest in Antarctica, it was announced that the southernmost continent would soon become a tourist destination: exclusively for travelers on the six-thousand-ton Norwegian *Stella Polaris*. Passengers would be able to see penguins and whales "without having to give up their armchairs, bathrooms with hot or cold water, bar, or dancing deck."

The published plan was to leave Southampton, England, for a 143-day tour around the world. Said the captain, Commander Joseph Russell Stenhouse: "We shall visit Admiral Byrd's old headquarters on the barrier, see Mount Erebus, the steaming volcano, and watch the great whaling fleets in action." Twelve clients signed on at first, setting aside a then astounding $2,500 to $6,500, with four women among that early dozen. If everything went as planned, they would be the first females ever to look upon the mighty barrier.

Commander Stenhouse soon admitted he was *deluged* with women the world over eager for adventure; considerably more than half of the applicants were female, to his surprise. At that news, even more women signed on, including the grieving Emily Dorman, the famous "Lady Shackleton," a widow desperate to connect to her lost hero husband. (Interestingly, according to the book *Ice Captain*, Stenhouse had captained the ship *Aurora* as part of Shackleton's 1914 expedition to the South Pole.) The corporate sponsors had found their unexpected market. Fifty women in all were to be on board a cruise that would leave December 10, 1930, with the ladies promised that they would be able to witness whales being electrocuted—a newfangled method of slaughter. The reality of the Depression soon killed this rather unique sightseeing excursion, but what a trip it would have been.

Billy's lecturing gig came to an end in August. What now? Where could he go from dead-whale handler? He wasn't a child anymore; he needed to help support his family in the faltering economy—but must he take whatever work came his way? Would he fritter away the rest of his life? His father had once desperately wanted him to get a degree, but how could Billy do that when he knew his family couldn't afford groceries? Maybe he could reapply to the tuition-free Cooper Union, but interior design was still not the path he saw for himself. He wanted to be an explorer. Sure, the expedition had not allowed him to overwinter, but he hadn't given up on his dreams. (And isn't that how nostalgia works? You forget the bitter cold and the backbreaking work and remember how happy you were playing with seals.)

Didn't Admiral Byrd tell him he needed a proper education to be a proper explorer? When Byrd selected the forty-one men to remain with him on the ice, he chose specialists in particular lines of work. Billy needed to master something useful. Something impressive.

Billy took three subways to the Columbia University campus in uptown Manhattan, one of the Ivy League universities that men like Byrd respected most. If accepted at Columbia, he could probably save costs by commuting from Bayside. That brought it into the realm of possibility, right?

He stared at the blank columns of the application form. Didn't Byrd write to contact him if he needed anything? A friendly administrator on campus had told Billy that a strong letter of recommendation would be essential. Who better to ask than Admiral Richard E. Byrd? But attending college to become an explorer would sound flaky, even to the world's foremost explorer. To approach Byrd for help, he must seem more levelheaded. On the spot, Billy decided he would apply to the university's dental school.

Only two problems remained: he would need a scholarship, and it was already September. The fall semester started that coming Thursday.

Even the admiral was having difficulty securing paying work for his expedition men, who were growing increasingly resentful of their years of unpaid heroism, now that they found themselves unable to support loved ones at home. The letters from staff were getting increasingly desperate, if never outright angry, but getting a kid admitted to Columbia was doable. A reference letter was penned to President Nicholas Murray Butler of Columbia University.

Byrd's letter did the trick: Billy got a partial scholarship as a twenty-year-old freshman. The university newspaper, the *Spectator*, deemed his admission the most exciting in the entire class of 451 incoming men. (There were no women at Columbia back then, a university only since 1896.) At a gathering of incoming freshmen in John Jay Hall, the boy explorer thrilled his new classmates with tales of his adventures; they broke out in applause when he promised to bring unreleased scientific films to campus. He soon pledged to the elite Sigma Alpha Upsilon fraternity.

Admiral Byrd visited campus in late September with his new illustrated lecture, "Exploring at the South Pole." McMillin Theatre held 1,300 people, and so great was demand for the "Only Man Who Flew to Both Ends of Earth" that he gave his talk twice. Most in the audience had seen the Paramount picture *With Byrd at the South Pole*, and, to his fans' delight, the adventurer brought out-takes. At both lectures, he called his old friend William Gawronski to the stage and wished him well on his academic studies at Columbia. The college boys cheered.

NINE

GREAT DEPRESSION

By 1932, if Billy wanted to return to Columbia, he would have to take off a semester, even with a partial scholarship. Rather than start his sophomore spring semester, he took a brief stint as a seaman on the SS *Leviathan*, the mammoth ship that had been docked next to the *New York* that night three and a half years earlier when he swam in the Hudson River to stow away. He'd save up some money and reenroll in the fall.

Some months before, after his freshman year, Billy had had second thoughts about committing to dentistry, and—again by letter—asked Byrd if he could help him get an internship with the American Museum of Natural History. He wanted to pursue studies that would make him a well-equipped naturalist. Byrd wrote to his good friend Dr. George H. Sherwood, the museum's curator in chief, who arranged for an unpaid internship. Billy read the letter at home. Unpaid? How had this backfired? His parents needed him to bring home dollars. He declined the internship.

When his tour aboard the *Leviathan* ended several months later, he resolved to try again. Billy wrote Byrd that he had resumed his search for a position ashore, especially at some museum or zoological institution, but that his attempts seemed futile. He implored the admiral for any leads on paying employment so that he could go back to school in the fall.

What could Byrd write? Everyone he had worked with was in his "greatest" financial peril, even him. He sent a note that he would keep Billy in mind.

Billy was not the only Gawronski writing to the admiral in the summer of 1932. Francesca, too, had struck up an epistolary exchange with the man, one of the strangest correspondences in Antarctic expedition history. Billy's meddling mother began this years-long exchange by needling Byrd first about her son's long-overdue medal, and then about whether he might do her the honor of autographing the book of newspaper clippings she had collected so fervently while her boy was at sea. She sent letter after letter when he failed to reply until his secretary told her to just send the damn album—which she did, along with pillows from the Gawronski upholstery business. (Billy knew about some of his mother's mortifying letters, but not all.)

Word soon leaked that Byrd was planning a second Antarctic expedition, and Billy could imagine himself in the running for a spot on the crew. He had been a sworn member of the Byrd Loyalty Club, had done everything asked of him without complaint. Should he write to Byrd again and formally ask to be considered? He did.

The economy continued to nose-dive through the fall, more than anyone thought possible. Apprehension was replaced by outright desperation. On November 24 the Soldiers and Sailors Club, a YMCA on the Hudson and an offshoot of the charitable Seamen's Church Institute, offered a free Thanksgiving meal well attended even by officers down on their luck—or, in unemployed-sailor parlance, "on the beach."

With little money in their pockets, Byrd's once-extolled men bumped into one another there—a chance reunion. Thirty-year-old second mate on the *Bolling*, Harry King, arrived first from Brooklyn; then in walked fifty-year-old Aussie Arthur "Hump" Creagh. Look! There was their favorite scamp, three inches taller and thirty pounds heavier than when they first met, finally more man than boy. (There was not much money for a Thanksgiving spread at the Gawronski home, and Billy's mother was a not-so-gentle nag, especially in these hard times.) Billy, knowing that King was a Columbia University graduate, must have told him he was a student now; the twenty-two-year-old had managed to scrape up enough to proceed with his sophomore year.

Thirty-year-old John Cody took a ferry from Staten Island and dropped in to the Seamen's Church Institute dining room, too. He'd been the *Bolling*'s genial first assistant engineer, livening the seas with stories of his early life on a Staten Island farm even when the *"Evermore Rolling"* seemed about to tip. It felt good to laugh again! The men remembered how Cody loved his monkey wrenches and coal shovels, kept under his bunk, near the mess room; they'd made a huge noise every time the ship pitched.

Over there! Another Byrd man cashing in on a free turkey meal: his stokehold buddy Kess with that special Black Gang bond from stoking the coals in unbearable heat. Yeah, Kess was still single, but at least he was living in New York—his overbearing mother having been left behind in DC.

Then, impossible! Isaac Erickson arrived. He'd come up from

Virginia as a hand on a ship, with no work to get back home. He knew Billy well and had traveled with Captain Melville after both were sent back to Dunedin, unnecessary in the winter months. They had returned to the barrier together in fierce storms to rescue the ones who'd stayed: men who were awarded gold medals despite having faced less danger.

A Seamen's Institute worker who watched the men all greet one another in shock and delight tipped off the Associated Press to what had to be a great story: six broke members of Byrd's illustrious expedition reduced to handouts. The Associated Press sent a man over.

"We'll get by," Creagh told the reporter who raced to the scene. "Times may be tough, but we are eating turkey again."

The reporter tried hard to end his piece on the struggling "Adventurous Six" optimistically, settling on, "High adventures every true adventurer always knows are waiting just beyond the horizon." Could he be right? Captain Brown had been living at the Seamen's Institute but wasn't there that Thanksgiving. Maybe the lucky could still find a paying stint at sea.

By the start of 1933, Rudy and Francesca were on the verge of losing their once-prosperous interior design business to bankruptcy, reduced to surviving off vegetables grown on a vacant lot next door, purchased cheaply and fortuitously in 1929. Rudy, like many breadwinners of this era, struggled to explain how this could have happened.

Billy could not in good conscience continue to drain his parents. Asking for Columbia University tuition, even if he lived at home on a partial scholarship, was perverse given the current financial woes. His folks had stood by him, and it was time to man up, do the right thing, and quit college. He would go back to the interior decorating business, help drum up sales, and then, when the family finances stabilized, return to school—whenever and wherever that might be. His parents wept openly but conceded he must quit.

However, even with his youthful energy, Billy could not save the family business. Fine upholstery work was not in demand in 1933.

With pennies to his name, he received an electrifying offer from the government of Poland asking the "Polish stowaway" to be a cadet on a Polish training ship, *Dar Pomorza*. He had to pass, though, again for financial reasons. A great honor would not pay the bills.

The offer nagged at him, but served as a reminder. Wasn't there always work for a good sailor? The officers on the *Leviathan* were thrilled that Billy did not have to be trained. A job at the port or at sea might not be Columbia University, but who cared at this point? He would get fed and be able to send cash home. Dishearteningly, Billy found even menial shipping jobs hard to come by, but the over-whelmed men assigning jobs on the dock brightened when he said that he'd worked in the dreaded stokehold. He was back to the dirty, hot jobs few people wanted, even in financial doom.

Billy gave it one last shot with the admiral, updating him on his employment woes (even stokehold jobs were few and far between; nothing approaching continuous employment)—and dropping a hint that he was available for Byrd's forthcoming second expedition. Then, just to cover all bases, he mentioned he had heard that after the March 4 inauguration of the thirty-second president of the United States, Franklin D. Roosevelt, who'd steamrolled incumbent Herbert Hoover in November, there would be many vacant positions in the US Department of Internal Revenue. Could the admiral intercede on his behalf with Mr. James A. Farley, the man he would need to see for such an appointment? A family friend who had introduced him in a celebratory dinner back in 1929, Edward C. Rybicki—director of the New York City Free Employment Bureau and a member of Polish Falcons Nest 7—had told his father that Farley was a powerful decision maker. He'd read that Byrd knew him.

This request did not sit well with the admiral. He was not going to use up his chits with someone like Farley over an ex-stowaway. The forty-five-year-old Farley was Roosevelt's influential campaign manager, often called a kingmaker, and one of the first Irish Catholics to achieve political success on a national level. (Today New York City's main post office, which stretches a block on Eighth Avenue, is named in his honor.)

Byrd was getting letters from every member of the expedition, and he'd just about had enough with these bullheaded Gawronskis. He tersely asked what experience Billy had for the job.

Experience? For a clerical job? "Jobs as Deputy Collectors require pure commonsense," Billy wrote back, elated, adding jocularly, in an increasingly rare glimpse of the goofy kid he once was, "perhaps I lack even that."

Perhaps he did. The admiral gave no reply.

Come April, and still no word, Francesca wrote to Byrd. (In shaky handwriting: you can almost feel the desperation holding the letter in your hands.)

At this point of the Depression, Byrd was ready to be guileless.

My dear Mrs. Gavronski,

On all of my expeditions and on two air stations, which I had command of during the war, I have had something like three or four hundred people who are in the same status with me as your son. I have gotten jobs for as many of these people as humanly possible and have spent a good part of my time doing so. So months ago, I used up all the influence I had and

have more or less reached the end of the rope in the matter of
getting jobs for my friends. As much as I would like to, I don't
know what I can do to get your son a position. If he will tell
me what to do, I will be glad to help or will give him a letter
of recommendation. As for getting a Government position
is concerned, it is impossible for me to do this. I am not a
politician and have no patronage to give out. I am very sorry,
indeed, Mrs. Gavronski.

Admiral Byrd

It was true. Byrd was increasingly stretched to the limits himself. He had put his second expedition on hold and volunteered to serve as chairman of the National Economic League, helping Roosevelt tackle the nation's growing poverty by reducing unnecessary governmental expenditures, which would in turn permit lower taxes. Heroism no longer required great feats of glory in far-off lands; it took getting the poor back to work. Hours of his day were devoted to the cause.

He was still trying to plan another expedition before polar explorer Lincoln Ellsworth—with plenty of experience at the top of the Earth, some of it partnered with the late Roald Amundsen—took off to Antarctica with Byrd's old pilot Bernt Balchen. (Balchen was by this time saying to all who'd listen that Byrd was a terrible navigator and that he himself had navigated the flights he'd flown over the South Pole.) With Balchen on his rival's team, Byrd was worried stiff that the Chicago-born Ellsworth would eclipse him as the hero of the Antarctic by making the first flight across the continent. Would Ellsworth's success erase Byrd's precious legacy?

The admiral was also busy developing a newsworthy attraction celebrating his Antarctic exploits for the 1933–34 Chicago World's

Fair, also known as the Century of Progress International Exposition. Byrd wanted to sign off on everything.

That summer, the genuine *City of New York* was set up as a walk-through attraction at the Michigan Avenue Bridge and Wacker Drive. Forty million Chicagoans and tourists went to see the Byrd exhibit, an ad hoc museum that housed a collection of historic relics, animal specimens, scientific instruments, cold-weather clothing, and dehydrated foods. There were dead animals galore on the old flagship, all taxidermied by the crew: penguins and skuas and an unborn baby whale. The Museum of Natural History spent $15,000 constructing a replica of Little America. It was good for public morale, Byrd justified. Former members of the expedition served as lecturers and guides. Harry Adams, grateful for any dollars in hard times, oversaw the attraction.

It was the Byrd World's Fair exhibit that introduced millions of American kids to the Antarctic. Shackleton and Scott get most of the glory, even today, but it was Richard Byrd who put the mysterious continent into America's popular consciousness.

Byrd's second expedition got under way that fall, financed by even more gifted goods than the first expedition and $150,000 in small donations doggedly raised in the middle of a Depression. The expedition is best remembered for the weekly radio broadcasts from Little America, with shortwave connections transmitted to Buenos Aires, Argentina, and from there to CBS studios in New York. If most of the crew found these casual scientific talks hokey, they were enormously popular back home, cementing Antarctica as part of American heritage.

This second expedition was a smaller undertaking than the first, with two ships, not four: the dainty barquentine *Bear of Oakland*

and the stout steel cargo vessel *Jacob Ruppert*. Billy did not swim to their side when they departed Boston for Dunedin, and no one tracked him down for comments. The Polish stowaway kid was old news, but three Kiwi stowaways were discovered on the *Bear* when it left Dunedin for the ice. All were allowed to stay on ship but, like Billy, not selected to overwinter.

Only the best and the brightest from the first expedition were asked back—or, one could say cynically, the men that Byrd felt least betrayed by. Of the seventy-one crewmen who journeyed on this second voyage to the Antarctic, eighteen were from the first. Those lucky enough to winter over included Paul Siple, now a biologist (as well as a dog driver), chief airplane pilot Harold June, meteorologist William Haines, and communications officer Charles Murphy.

Billy was privately devastated to read that Siple was asked along, but it was actually a wise decision on Byrd's part. The ex–Boy Scout became an accomplished explorer, authored four books, and coined the term *windchill factor*. After Byrd, his would be the most significant name in US polar history.

And Billy? It was almost as if he had never been on Byrd's first expedition at all. He was still in touch with Harry Adams, but less so. He had even drifted from his childhood friends who knew him back when he was obsessed with Byrd. There was hardly anyone around anymore to remind him of his grand, forsaken hope for a life of significance.

The Columbia University dropout lifted himself out of despair with a plan hatched at four in the morning: instead of becoming a dentist or an explorer, or a worker bee on a dreary nine-to-five, he would become an officer in the US Merchant Marines. It was the only foreseeable future with any promise of adventure; a compromise between the realities of adulthood and his adolescent dreams. Since 1775, the

Merchant Marines have been a civilian fleet senior to all the armed forces, transferring cargo and passengers in peacetime and military personnel and matériel in war. Billy studied to be an officer at home and in night school, after days of swabbing decks or working any odd job he could find in Bayside sweeping floors. In February 1936 he received his third mate license, issue 2114986—No. 016452. If he found employment as such, he would be a safety officer and fourth in command.

But there were no third mate jobs to be had. Billy did enough asking at the dock to sign on as a general seaman with several of the ships he hoped to one day become an officer of, such as the SS *Manhattan*, traveling regularly between New York and Hamburg, Germany. In July he was aboard the *Manhattan* when it left Pier 60 with 334 members of the US Olympic team, a vigorous group on its way to Nazi Germany to compete in the eleventh Olympic Games, presided over by Adolf Hitler in Berlin. In a ship commandeered to be a floating gym, Billy met dozens of athletes, perhaps even track-and-field great Jesse Owens, a black man who would infuriate Hitler by winning four gold medals at the Games, or runner Louis Zamperini—the spirited athlete who would be later shot down over the Pacific, his story told in Laura Hillenbrand's bestselling book *Unbroken*. As a US Army Air Forces bomber pilot in 1943, his plane was shot down; he and two crewmates drifted at sea for nearly seven weeks before being captured by the Japanese. (One of the three died during the ordeal at sea.) Zamperini spent the rest of the war under harsh conditions in prison camps in Japan. Billy was six years older than Zamperini but his equal in verve. Perhaps these two young men found each other on board during the long passage across the Atlantic.

In 1937 Billy got his first officer assignment as an extra third mate on the *Manhattan*. He would never forget the quietly haunting discussions he had that year with Jewish first-class clientele fleeing the Third Reich by ocean liner, already fearing the worst. Surprisingly, the Nazis encouraged this exit of Jewish elites to remove leadership and alienate the world against Jews begging entry to foreign lands. On the *Manhattan*, the young Polish officer spoke to the fleeing Jews in German; when the conversation turned sobering, he switched to perfect Yiddish. Like the parents who had hired him to be a Lower East Side *Shabbos* goy, the Jewish passengers were dumbfounded that the Polish American spoke their secret tongue. They were lucky to get out, they told him; others were being rounded up, and disappearing, and laws were being instated that prevented them from going about their lives. What a conflict he felt, an American who knew too much. Billy cried openly when in June 1939 the SS *St. Louis* sent back Jewish German refugees who had made it nearly to Miami. The ship had originally headed to Havana, but immigration officers there accepted only 29 of the 937 desperate passengers, and requests for mercy to the United States were turned down.

Passengers Jewish and Gentile told the commanding officers to look out for that young man Gawronski, a treasure. The captain liked the fellow already; he came experienced, pleasant, and, most importantly, deferential. Captain Harry Manning had a word with Billy. Had he ever considered becoming a sea captain?

The thought hadn't really crossed his mind. It took proper schooling to attain a position of significance. Hadn't Byrd taught him that? Wasn't that why he had impoverished his parents in pursuit of that abandoned Ivy League degree? But no. No. He thought back to the kindly Captain Brown, with no more than a high school education to his name. You just had to be scrappy, that was all. When you got caught on the *New York*, you tried again on the *Bolling*. Surely Billy knew that.

At last his run of bad luck seemed behind him. At the tail end of the Depression, late in 1939, twenty-nine-year-old Billy obtained his first master's license (which qualified him to become a captain) and joined the Alcoa Steamship Company of Weehawken, New Jersey, to work on vessels of the Hog Island type, made at the shipyards of Hog Island in Pennsylvania, now replaced with Philadelphia International Airport, and then engaged in Caribbean and South American trade. His initial assignment was as second officer. Not even a year later, he was chief mate, sailing out of San Francisco on the SS *Yarmouth*. Under the prewar authority of the US military, the ship had a "Caribbean" route—although it also served Newfoundland, Labrador, and Greenland—transporting a combination of cargo and soldiers even before the 1941 Japanese attack on Pearl Harbor that catapulted the United States into World War II.

Soon after he showed up in San Francisco, he secured temporary living quarters on Gough Street and began frequenting a nearby bar. He had his eye on another regular: a twenty-three-year-old nurse named Goldy Mundy, a tarty type never without the reddest lipstick and often accompanied by her older sister, also a nurse and also at ease with the men at the bar. Despite Goldy's loose reputation with the regulars, he asked her to dinner. He was in great spirits, making real money now as an officer, and he had a hot date who made other women nervous and men a little jealous.

Rudy had never been able to get his interior decoration business going again, and now the rising Billy wanted to use his contacts to help his father's career—a means of atonement for being the irresponsible young'un he was. The Merchant Marines were planning a new academic facility, with offices in the once-luxurious 1920s Chrysler Mansion in a wealthy enclave of Long Island called Kings Point, the inspiration for the fictional West Egg in F. Scott Fitzgerald's *The Great Gatsby*. With a letter from Billy, Rudy got a secure government job at the US Merchant Marine Academy, his title head of interior decoration. (He would be proud of his effort here, especially as he witnessed the building's dedication by President Franklin D. Roosevelt in 1943; Rudy's handiwork was in every room the president visited. Today you can still see the upholstered sides of the campus chapel, although none of Rudy's much-admired curtain work remains.)

Across the country in San Francisco, things heated up between Billy and Goldy, that spicy gal. She was four years younger than him, flushed with youth and the exhilaration of ditching her strict religious parents back in Friendship, Illinois. On every date, she sported tantalizing clothes that soon came off. His friends didn't love her—didn't even like her—but to this bachelor officer open to adventure, and with the first bit of extra cash in his pocket in a long while, she was the opposite of a stick-in-the-mud. She even outranked him: a nurse captain and her chief mate. Billy liked that about her: a woman who let him know she was important. Yet his friends pressed him to drop her. But Billy was smitten.

His parents were alarmed to learn by letter that she might be the one, remembering all too well how rashly he had talked of marrying his senior-year girlfriend in high school. But Billy couldn't stop thinking about her. With his encouragement, Goldy wrote to his mother as if this woman she'd never met were already her new mother-in-law, addressing her as "Dear Mother Gawronski."

Well, Francesca admitted to Rudy, she seemed polite enough on the page.

Richard Byrd no longer had to fund-raise to conduct an expedition south. For his third expedition to the Antarctic, from 1939 to 1941, he worked with the US Navy, the State Department, the Department of the Interior, and the Treasury—federal agencies that covered most of the costs. This was America's first government-sponsored expedition, authorized by Byrd's old friend President Roosevelt and known formally as the US Antarctic Service Expedition. The many objectives included establishing two permanent bases and mapping the continent's mostly unknown west coast.

There were 125 men—a proper expedition this time—some civilian scientists but mostly navy personnel. Former Boy Scout Paul Siple was selected for his third trip with Byrd—the only man from the first Antarctic expedition to return—and was put in charge of the West Base (at the Bay of Whales) party of twenty-nine overwinterers. East Base, on Stonington Island, was 2,200 miles away by sea. Lesser known was twenty-three-year-old George Gibbs, a native of Jacksonville, Florida, and a navy man added to the expedition as a mess boy. Gibbs may have been peeling potatoes to pay his way, but he fulfilled the dream that Robert White Lanier had been chasing for almost a decade: On January 14, 1940, he became the first black man to walk in Antarctica. Admiral Byrd shook his hand and welcomed him to Little America.

There were no scrapbooks of Byrd's third expedition in the Gawronski household. Billy was off on his own adventures. At great risk, still as a Merchant Marine, he served a stint as chief mate on a ship making a charity food drop to an extraordinary orphanage in East Africa, run by Franciscan monks in the hills of northern Tanganyika (now Tanzania), fifty miles from Mount Kilimanjaro at the foot of sloping, wooded fifteen-thousand-foot-high Mount Meru, Africa's fifth-highest mountain. The orphanage was populated with several hundred once-malnourished Polish youngsters who had survived the Siberian Gulags, where a million soldiers, intellectuals, and other civilians had been sent with their families following the Soviet invasion of Poland in September 1939. Many did not survive the brutality of the camps, and the children who were lucky enough to be released before long were shipped to faraway places such as India and Africa to recuperate.

Billy had a way with courageous, vivacious kids. He had learned of the tragic foundlings from his Polish family and church, and was grateful to be part of a team bringing supplies. He was especially playful with a boy who called himself Tarzan. The chief mate, too, thumped his chest, whooping and climbing trees in a tangle of agave and cacti, while the orphans—hidden away in huts and barracks near safari grounds—giggled. Here was a man in an officer's uniform bringing candy; a kind American who could speak to the children in their own language about the country far away where they made movies and no one starved.

This adventure was more rewarding than others he'd had in the past, Billy would say later—more human—but he still had a thrill-seeking itch that wouldn't go away.

Jan Paderewski, the most famous living Pole, died in exile in New York in June 1941. The news greatly saddened Billy, who, as a boy, had recited a poem before him in his Lower East Side church; his lifelong love of poetry started there. He was always impressing people with how many poems he had memorized and would pack volumes of poetry for long sea journeys. Billy's favorite poets were the Romantics: William Wordsworth, Samuel Taylor Coleridge, Percy Shelley, and especially John Keats. On his own adventures now, he no longer read voraciously about those of others but instead about the intricacies of love and loss.

In a letter to his parents from sea en route to Hawaii, dated August 18, 1941, Billy said that Goldy was very proud of her engagement ring.

On December 7 the Japanese attacked Pearl Harbor, and Billy was soon hired by the State Marine Lines of 90 Broad Street in New York

City to serve on Liberty ships—the ugly ducklings so synonymous with this era. These assembly-line wartime vessels were built on the cheap in record time, sometimes in a matter of days, with women often welding alongside men.

The US Merchant Marines were civilians, not military men, yet they suffered the worst casualties of World War II without any of the glory and veteran's benefits of their countrymen in the army, navy, and army air forces. In February 1942 Adolf Hitler thundered on the radio that US Merchant Marines were fools and would die a certain death. He was not that much of a liar, on this matter, at least. The waters were treacherous, especially for ships commandeered for cargo—cargo oftentimes more of a target than the men serving aboard.

On March 2 the South African petrol tanker *Uniwaleco* (formerly the Norwegian-built whaler *Sir James Clark Ross* that in 1928 had carried Arthur Walden and his nearly one hundred dogs as far as New Zealand) was torpedoed by a German submarine, or U-boat, in the Caribbean. Most of the men made it to lifeboats, but a follow-up strike sank the ship. Almost all of the men on life rafts were killed in subsequent attacks, with the two men remaining in the rear of the ship blown to bits.

Billy's run was farther north, to ice-free Murmansk, a port city in the Soviet Union. Hitler had betrayed his treaty with Russian leader Joseph Stalin, launching a massive surprise assault in 1941. The reckless tactic not only drove Stalin into the arms of the Allies but also mired the German army in the east. At Murmansk, the US Merchant Marines unloaded manufactured goods and raw materials to help the fearless Russian fighters repel German troops from the Eastern front. However, big convoys sailing from Halifax, Nova Scotia, to Murmansk were regularly preyed upon by Nazi U-boats. Eighty-five ships were lost en route, and hundreds more in other runs across the North Atlantic. One out of every twenty-six men died. Newspapers ran the same story each week: "Two Medium-Sized Allied Ships Sunk in the Atlantic." In reality, the averages for 1942 were thirty-three Allied ships sunk every week—or one out of every four—8,500 Merchant Marines killed, and another 11,000 wounded.

Billy would say later that these terrifying runs to Murmansk were the defining experiences of his life, even more than his adventures in Antarctica. He considered himself lucky; he never broke down from the memories, like other survivors he knew. But Billy would never talk much about those days. Some adventures are best left unexamined.

Billy had occasional home leave, but his home life back in Bayside, near his parents, was far from peaceful. By the summer of 1942, after less than a year of marriage, he was determined to divorce. There was nonstop fighting; at times he found Goldy downright mean. She mimicked his parents' accents and mocked his love of Polish food. She threw dishes against the wall and broke precious antiques he had picked out—souvenirs from cherished journeys around the world. He knew he had made a dreadful mistake and told Goldy it was over. But his young wife had news for him: she was pregnant.

On February 20, 1943, Goldy Gawronski gave birth to the unhappy couple's first of two sons, William Gregory Gawronski, always called Billy Jr. The new father looked for a landlubber assignment so he could stay close to his growing family. A younger Billy might have run, shipping off across the globe to escape unpleasantness at home. But war had taught him responsibility. Still, there was a dearth of qualified sailing masters, which weighed on him, too. Wasn't it his obligation and his honor to serve his country, especially in this time of war?

When Billy Jr. was barely two months old, his father, at the extraordinarily young age of thirty-two, was offered his own Liberty ship. She would be built for him in Wilmington, North Carolina, by Cape Fear Shipping Company at Custom House Brokers and Steamship Agents on 713 Nutt Street. A letter arrived with her name: he read it to Goldy at their home. If Billy said yes, he would be the master of the SS *Jose Bonifacio*, transporting men and cargo to all theaters of war: Atlantic, Pacific, and Mediterranean. The ship, he later found out, was named for "the patriarch of Brazilian independence," José Bonifácio.

He called the Cape Fear Shipping offices at tel 2-3892 and got a checklist of what had to be done. And then, in the privacy of his room, Billy wept. He said yes. The stowaway would become captain of his own ship.

Billy was one of the youngest captains in World War II. He ordered a silver bracelet etched with "Captain William G. Gawronski," the type worn by American Merchant Marines in war zones, and settled on a captain's hat made by Wallachs, of Fifth Avenue, treated with Gravanette (patent pending) to repel water in the almost inevitable storms. Word was the *Bonifacio* would load out of Charleston, South Carolina, off to India for at least a six-month trip.

But first a letter to his parents was in order before he left South Carolina. He signed it with:

"All my love, and regards to all, Captain Bill Gawronski."

His signature was *big and proud* and underlined.

EPILOGUE

William Gawronski never returned to Antarctica. He was missing from the fourth and final Byrd expedition, code-named Operation Highjump, which immediately followed World War II. In many respects, it was a military operation to protect America's position as the most powerful country on the global stage. Admiral Byrd, now head of the US Navy's Antarctic Developments Program, had a significant detachment at his disposal: thirteen navy support ships, six helicopters, six flying boats, two seaplane tenders, and fifteen other aircraft, as well as four thousand personnel. The expedition, by far the largest to date, explored the eastern coastline of Antarctica by air, an area roughly half the size of the United States. They charted ten new mountain ranges.

Billy was not invited to take part in this expedition for the same reason he had not been invited on Byrd's second or third. It was not, as Billy had feared for years, in anger and confusion, because he had somehow failed to prove his worth. No. It was because of concern.

Billy knew his mother had written to Byrd at least once following the first expedition, but he would never know that Francesca Gawronski had secretly written the admiral more than a dozen times between 1931 and 1933. She knew how her son longed to return to the South Pole—how eagerly he would drop his studies at Columbia for two more years on ice and on sea—and she knew, too, should he do so, how unlikely it was that he would ever finish his degree. She would support her son becoming an adventurer, but not a mess boy or a coal passer to the end of his days. So in the summer of 1932, as rumors of a second expedition swirled, she penned a desperate letter to Byrd, begging him not to take her son away. "It is our desire to see Bill attain something better and higher in life," she wrote, speaking for her husband as well as herself. "He is our only son, and we see in him an ideal."

Byrd replied, with a parent's understanding, for he had been a surrogate father to the boy for two years: "I will do exactly as you wish me to in regard to your son. I will promise you not to take him even if he stows away."

Although Billy never saw Antarctica again, his two years with the Byrd expedition altered the course of his life. The expedition provided an escape from the dreary future in his father's upholstery business that had seemed so unavoidable at seventeen. It introduced him to a world of danger and discovery that had existed only in his scrapbooks and library loans, and gave him the basic seaman's training with which he made a career.

After two years as the master of the SS *Bonifacio*—and with many treacherous runs, including the dreaded North Atlantic, that he was lucky to survive—Billy returned home to a country at peace.

But he could not stay. War had cured him of his reckless thrill seeking, but not his love for the sea.

He would spend the next decades in the Merchant Marines, traveling to every continent but the one he'd visited first. Every port he landed in, he would alight and explore. Once, in Bombay, India, he was led down tiny streets to an antique trader's shop and left to find his way back to the docks on foot, hiding his precious buys among his clothes. Sailing to Taipei, Taiwan, he sipped tea in an alleyway before he was trusted enough to bring carved jade antiquities back to the ship. In the Italian port of Gioia Tauro, he was invited to dine in a local home, the captain's privilege, and was served octopus so hard that he discreetly slipped the tentacles in his pockets before being asked to dance.

These later journeys certainly weren't as glamorous as his first—no newsies clamoring for a scoop, no tickertape parades on his return— yet he found them more satisfying. Often Billy was saving lives in communities suffering from famine or drought. When the Vietnam War raged in the 1960s and early 1970s, he answered his country's call once again, carrying cargo for the US Military Sealift Command.

Billy had poems all over his ships, memorized every sailor's name on day one, and never drank at sea—though he did smoke like a chimney, a habit picked up from the free Chesterfield cigarettes offered on the *Bolling*. In later years, he would tack his favorite poem—"Dreams of the Sea," written by William Henry Davies in 1913—on the bulletin boards of many of the ships he commanded, for all crew to read:

> *I know now why I yearn for thee again*
> *To sail once more upon thy fickle flood*
> *I'll hear thy waves under my death bed*
> *Thy salt is lodged forever in my blood.*

It was his hero, Richard Byrd, who had lodged that salt in his blood the September day he let Billy stay aboard the *Eleanor Bolling* after his third attempt to stow away, Byrd who had enabled the decades of adventure that were to come. For that, Billy would always be grateful.

And yet for all his grand adventures, the stowaway found himself longing for home.

Billy met the young antiques shop manager Gizela Trawicka while abroad in Gdańsk, Poland, in 1958. He popped into a curio shop while his ship was at dock and happened upon the love of his life. On their first date, she laughed as he told her about himself; she had learned about Admiral Byrd's Polish stowaway in her history class. Billy was divorced by this time (yes, his split with Goldy was inevitable), and after a passionate courtship—a few blissful days of art and theater and restaurants, an introduction to Gizela's widowed mother—followed by a year of tender letters to "my Gizeluchna," he returned to Poland to marry Gizela in a small church ceremony. It would take another year for the US government to grant permission for Gizela to emigrate to New York State.

Billy, by then fifty, cried as she stepped off her ship in September 1960 onto a pier jutting into the same Hudson River from which he had set off on his own adventure so long ago. He was ashamed to bring her home to an old house on a sandy, horseshoe-shaped patch of land, once part of an estate belonging to the shipbuilding Lilly family, in Northport, Long Island's heyday. He'd snatched up the acres on the cheap in the postwar years, and it was now the last ramshackle parcel he had been able to hold on to after the divorce. Gizela assured him that they would fix it up together and turn it into a home.

How odd it was for both of them to feel happy after all these years! She had lost part of one arm to World War II shrapnel, and had spent the days since then in hunger and in grief, and the nights sleeping on a couch at the back of her antiques store. For him, there were bitter memories of a first marriage that no amount of adventure could make him forget.

Like anyone in love, Billy wanted to show his bride his history. They shopped for peppery kielbasa in the remaining Polish delis of the Lower East Side—so many had moved away, and now there were turtle-necked beatniks everywhere. He took Gizela to the Seamen's Institute and explained how the men there had helped him ride out the roughest days of the Depression, and about the day he unexpectedly ate Thanksgiving dinner with so many of his old friends.

The two were perfect for each other, each marveling at the other's kindness. They spent happy evenings preparing favorite Polish recipes and eating by candlelight in their kitchen that Billy had sketched to look like a ship's galley and then manifested into reality through his own woodworking skills. They shared a love of antiques and visited museums to take in art exhibits. They joined a Polish church.

The couple never had children; Gizela did not want to bring youngsters into a world where there was war.

In bed one night, Billy asked Gizela to share her secret dreams for her future. She admitted that she had wanted to be an artist but never had the opportunity to pursue this in Gdańsk. Soon she was taking the Long Island Railroad into Manhattan once a week to study Oriental art under artist and collector Warren E. Cox, a longtime arts editor for *Encyclopædia Britannica* and author of the most respected books in the field.

Gizela didn't mind Billy's voyages; they gave her time alone to paint. But after each two-month-long stint at sea, she would meet him at the wharves, arms outstretched. How funny that something that had played no part in his adolescent dreams now seemed to be precisely what made life so worth living.

He and Gizela opened a nursery with a roadside stand and a greenhouse that Billy had bought at auction and restored himself. The newly christened Buttonwood Farms specialized in broadleaf evergreens, shrubs, ground cover, rock and dwarf plants, and other rare botanicals Billy loved to research, channeling the scientists on his long-ago Antarctica trip. At the Eighteenth Annual Northport Veterans Fall Flower and Vegetable Show in 1964, Buttonwood Farms won the gold medal in three categories, which Billy said to his wife felt almost as good as getting another Congressional Medal of Honor. Before long, the plants were moved out of the greenhouse so they could expanded the business, now rechristened Buttonwood Antiques.

In 1972, while on assignment to reactivate an old steel trawler for commercial fishing in Portland, Maine, Billy fell in love with the area: the lighthouses, the exquisite light. The following year, he and Gizela retired to a fixer-upper in the nearby community of Cape Elizabeth. And so the stowaway found himself living out his days not on the windswept, desolate Ross Ice Barrier but happily toiling away in his own verdant backyard. The orange California poppies everywhere were his pride, an unexpected burst of joy for strangers passing by. There, amidst the poppies, purple veronica, mountain pinks, Siberian irises, and thyme, Billy the stowaway rediscovered each day the joys of being home.

AUTHOR'S NOTE

Although the story of Billy Gawronski reads like that of some character sprung from the pages of Robert Louis Stevenson or Mark Twain
and plunked down in twentieth-century New York City—between
world wars, at the height of the Jazz Age—it is a work of nonfiction.
After stumbling upon his name while researching a possible article on
Manhattan's St. Stanislaus Parish on East Seventh Street, the oldest Polish Catholic church in America, I became obsessed with the Polish kid
stowaway. I was desperate for more source material. I didn't know yet
that the 1920s newspaper article I'd read had misspelled his last name
"Gavronski," with a *v*, but I had a hunch that back then reporters often
struggled with long foreign names. Trying phonetic variations, I found
another mention, and then yet another and another, and, at last, a larger
story emerged. Gawronski had been, as I hoped, all over the news!

Searching online cemetery listings, I found a William Gawronski
with a birth year that matched his age. This William Gawronski died in

Maine. I had been cold-calling Gawronskis up and down the East Coast to laughable results, but now I tried a woman in Maine, possibly a descendant. The elderly lady who answered had an accent, and was clearly not a daughter or granddaughter. I apologized for the morning intrusion, explaining that in 1928 a boy had swum the Hudson to stow away to Antarctica; I hoped there might be a family connection. The woman said, "That boy was my husband. My name is Gizela Gawronski."

Billy had died in 1981. By choice, Gizela had never remarried; nor had she gotten rid of her deceased husband's many mementoes—including his childhood scrapbook and notebooks devoted to the exploits of Commander Richard Byrd. She also held on to souvenirs from the expedition, such as a paper cup decorated with icebergs and huskies and a pack of Chesterfield cigarettes; only later did I grasp their significance.

The first Byrd expedition to Antarctica was in its time a major event in American history. But as the years passed, people forgot the then household names of the sixty-odd men on the journey: the ship captains, the first mates, and the stowaway. Then, for the most part, they even forgot Admiral Byrd.

Gizela had hoped there would be a way to put these saved materials to good use before it was too late for her as well. She had spent many a day and night discussing her husband's astounding past with him and kindly invited me into her home. I was there within the week. Over several visits in her kitchen, we went through the old family scrapbooks and his notebooks, and hundreds of photos of Billy and his family: in a sailor suit at three; with his first love from high school; as a dashing young Merchant Marine. Gizela allowed me to photocopy her archives at her local packing store. In addition to hours of recorded in-person discussions, we spoke dozens of times between visits. To date, she still has never tried email.

A few months later, a Google Alert for "William Gawronski" went off, and I was baffled by a mugshot that looked like the kid stowaway as an older man. (I held a photocopy from Gizela's house next to the screen.) Billy's wife believed that her two troubled but bright stepsons had been dead for many years after getting caught up in 1960s drug culture and then lives of crime. George, the younger son, *was* dead, but William, the elder, was facing a thirty-year sentence in northern Florida for a drug-related crime. His photo had been published online because he was fighting for parole. (He lost. It's hard to overturn a stiff Florida jail term even with years of exemplary behavior and advanced age.) After many letters and phone calls, and after reassuring his defense attorneys and wardens that I would stick to questions about American polar history, I was granted permission to visit a high-security prison deep in orange-grove territory. According to one warden, Billy Jr. had been startled to hear from me and was eager to meet. I was his first visitor in years.

In his orange jumpsuit, Billy Jr. told me he had tremendous guilt about his past. He welcomed the opportunity to answer my questions, and I soon found he had an astonishing memory, just like Billy Sr. Over the visits and letters and phone calls, Billy Jr. offered new details about his father, his grandparents, and even his tiny great-grandmother, who showed him her amulets and crystal ball that, according to her, had predicted his father's future. Gizela had never met her husband's in-laws or his beloved grandmother, but Billy Jr. knew them all well. I later fact-checked the two accounts against each other and was relieved to find no conflicts, although each had salty details the other lacked. Billy Jr. also offered me particulars about World War II that his father had shared with him as a young boy that surprised experts in the field but turned out to hold weight. I've never had reason to doubt his important contributions to my research.

It is easier to write about the beauty of Antarctica's Ross Ice Barrier when you have reached it yourself after a violent storm and have watched great chunks break off and float out to sea. And it is easier to write about early flight over the iciest yet most startlingly polychromatic continent when you have flown above it in a helicopter yourself. So despite my considerable fear of seasickness, I traveled by ship for a monthlong visit to what is still the most mysterious continent. I hope I have imbued the thrill of that once-in-a-lifetime experience into this story of a brave boy that was, until now, lost to history.

Laurie Gwen Shapiro, New York, 2017

ACKNOWLEDGMENTS

My first nonfiction book, spanning more than a hundred years of history, was a vast undertaking, and many people helped bring it to fruition.

First and foremost, I'd like to thank Gizela Gawronski, Billy's widow from his second marriage, who was with me on this journey from our first phone contact. I am so very grateful to her.

William Gawronski Jr. was a most unexpected source of information, and I thank him as well for his quick attention to any questions I had. As he remains jailed, this is no small feat.

Much gratitude goes to my phenomenal editor, Megan Hogan, who surpassed my expectations. Every email from her brings a smile to my face.

Simon & Schuster's publisher, Jonathan Karp, was an early champion as well as executive editor Priscilla Painton. Their expert feedback also helped shape this narrative greatly. Much appreciation also goes to Thomas LeBien (who bought the book on proposal in 2013) and

Millicent Bennett, early editorial stewards. Thanks also to Simon & Schuster's Anne Pearce, Jessica Breen, Jackie Seow, Ruth Lee-Mui, Philip Bashe, Chelsea Cohen, Allison Har-zvi, Pete Garceau, and Marie Florio.

Gratitude goes to my cherished agent Holly McGhee of Pippin Properties, who took over when my (equally adored) agent Julie Just retired from the business to focus on writing—but, fortunately, not until just after Julie's sale of my book. My deepest appreciation also goes to Robin Budd from Viewfinder Management for her skillful guidance and emotional support throughout the writing of this book.

Byrd expedition historian Eugene Rodgers gave me a marvelous in-person interview early on, and I sent him countless emails clarifying new information (as his research was done before the internet era), which he always replied to within minutes. It was like having a Talmudic scholar on call.

Exceptional help was also offered in person (and online for several years) by Laura Kissel, Ohio State University's Byrd polar historian.

Much thanks to Iwona Korga of the Józef Piłsudski Institute of America, and her volunteer assistant Agnieszka Petla Brissey, who served as my Polish translator there. In a wonderful coincidence, while at the Piłsudski Institute, I mentioned that I needed to go to the Merchant Marine Academy in Kings Point, New York, and met Agnieszka's graduating fiancé (now husband), Ian Brissey, who led me on a daylong tour of the academy, set up interviews with his instructors there, and helped me find relics of Rudolf Gawronski's original interior decorating.

Heather Davis drove me around her neighborhood of Bayside—a perfect excuse to spend time with an old high school friend. Jonathan Sherman drove me around Columbus, Ohio—a perfect excuse to spend time with an old elementary school friend.

As you may gather, my native New Yorker's lack of driver's license is a theme here. When I needed to visit a prison deep in orange-grove territory, I asked Alan Solowitz of Tampa, one of the two adopted sons of the "Jewish stowaway" Jack Solowitz (featured in this narrative), if he'd like to drive me, and I could interview him en route. Thus the warring stowaways' sons were reunited almost ninety years after their fathers' quarrel led to their discovery. Alan has since become a friend.

Celebrated activist swimmer Lewis Pugh did his remarkable five Speedo polar swims on my 2015 Ross Sea journey to bring attention to the wildlife of the Ross Sea. Lewis was a wonderful dinner companion and, when not shivering, a trusted source on describing swimming in open water.

There were many other experts on my 2015 expedition that I also peppered with questions at dinnertime, including James Creswell on geology, and Jim Mayer on Shackleton, and Antarctica historian Carol Knott. Dr. Gary Miller, one of the foremost penguin experts in the world, was also a mentor on this trip, and he insisted I reach the Ross Barrier by inflatable rubber Zodiac seacraft on the worst weather day of the trip. I'll never forget as he sang to calm his five passengers who risked the experience, as we were frozen and terrified, and briefly the six humans on the southernmost vessel in the world. During this monthlong expedition, I also befriended Anne Charlesworth and Karina Taylor, two veteran travelers to Antarctica, who talked this chicken into many more Zodiac and helicopter trips even in iffiest weather. My greatest companion on the journey was the oldest passenger on the ship, Sam Adams, who thrilled me with stories of visiting the Byrd exhibit at the Chicago World's Fair (Century of Progress) in 1934 and who remains a dear friend.

A special shout-out to genealogist Kenyatta Berry of PBS's *Genealogy Roadshow*, as she helped me trace African American stowaway Robert White Lanier, who proved one of the more frustrating characters to follow, as he disappeared from the historical record after the 1930s.

Eric Pomerance, my former writing partner, offered a careful read-through of the manuscript, a sharp-eyed review of my promotional materials, and much emotional support, and Corey S. Powell, in addition to a read-through, drove this desperate New Yorker without a license to Cape Elizabeth, Maine, for my first interview with Billy Gawronski's widow.

My close friends Maria Smilios and Sarah Rose, who are my

talented and motivated nonfiction support gals, offered daily encouragement throughout the writing of the book.

My husband, Paul O'Leary, took care of our daughter, Violet O'Leary, when I was away in Antarctica. And vice versa. The ability to go all out was essential for me to tell the story. Thank you both for the extraordinary gift of time and love.

Additional thanks to Captain Kenneth R. Force, USMS; Father Lizinczyk, St. Stanislaus Church; Johnathan Thayer, Seamen's Church Institute; Dan Brenner, Queens College Library; Lacey Flint, the Explorers Club; George Billy, chief librarian, US Merchant Marine Academy; Larry Solowitz; Maryanne Smolka, who generously let me tour Billy Gawronski's former Bayside home where she lives now; Steven King of the Northport Historical Society; celebrated author Tom Reiss and New York City historian and author James Sanders, both of whom were advocates of the book in its proposal stage; Northport enthusiast Vicki Karp; Florida district attorney Debra Munchel, who helped fight for access to William Gawronski Jr.; Conor McCourt, who ran private investigator reports of Billy's sons for me; Ann and Susan Beyer, daughters of Frederick Beyer, Billy Gawronski's closest friend as an adult; Billy Gawronski's former third mate Captain Earl Mealins; Cape Elizabeth historian Barbara Sanborn; Bayside historian Alison McKay; radio historian Dr. Donna Halper; Alec Cumming; Janet Rosen, who has the photo-captioning gene I was not born with; the talented Franco Vogt for taking my author photo in his Woodstock studio; Lucia Reale-Vogt; Adam Lawrence, for his photo-clearance expertise; Pam Swing, who introduced me to Eleanor "Lee" Byrd; Dona Siatras; the Merchant Marines historian, Joshua M. Smith; and Ainslie Heather, Port Chalmers librarian.

NOTES

Much of the daily activities of the Byrd campaign, before, during, and afterward, were covered by the *New York Times*, official paper of the expedition. Unless noted, general expedition details come from that coverage, which was generally accurate although not impartial. Commander Byrd, for example, was never disparaged. Many other newspapers of the era were consulted, but the *Times*'s star journalist Russell Owen was along for the journey and received a Pulitzer Prize for his coverage. Please assume that general expedition details come from this widely available coverage, which, for the most part, if left unchallenged, were backed by eminent Byrd scholars such as Eugene Rodgers and his colleague Lisle A. Rose. If my original research later disproved information or uncovered new details not covered by those scholars, like a cow being sent to Antarctica from Los Angeles, I was privileged to run it by my (now friend) Eugene Rodgers, who would debate me as to whether it was a legitimate add. We did not always agree but always had fun debating.

In-person and phone interviews form the core of personal information on William Gawronski; the most useful were with his second wife, Gizela Gawronski, and his son William Gawronski Jr.

Gizela Gawronski is GG.

William Gawronski Jr. is WG Jr.

The deceased Francesca Gawronski, whose motherly scrapbooks proved invaluable as well, is FG.

Byrd scholar Eugene Rodgers is ER.

PROLOGUE

1 *three inches short*: 1928 Ohio BAE 1, file 4876; 1930s and 1940s resumes; and William Gawronski death certificate.

2 *"You are a late bloomer"*: Interview with GG.

2 *The 161-foot wooden vessel . . . 34 inches thick*: City of New York boat measurements come from multiple sources, including the 1930 *New York Times* celebratory booklet *The Barque "City of New York,"* by Russell Owen.

2 *Nine days earlier*: Copy of Billy Gawronski's 1929 speech at Textile High School.

7 *A few minutes past four in the morning*: Written copy of speech for radio address on WOR, April 24, 1929.

ONE: THE GOLDEN DOOR

9 *Billy's future father . . . Ellis Island*: Rudolf Gawronski immigration details are from naturalization and shipping records.

9 *East Eighteenth Street*: Old letters, collection of GG.

9 *he'd courted pretty fifteen-year-old Fromia Zajac*: Interview with GG.

10 *Deutsch Brothers*: Old letters, collection of GG.

11 *57 First Avenue*: New York City marriage license.

11 *An alderman at city hall wed*: Ibid.

12 *SS Patricia*: Photos, correspondence in collection of GG.

13 *the Polish Falcons*: Much of this historical information was drawn from Larry Wroblewski, "Polish Falcons: A Historical Stretch," *Polish American Journal*, July 1985.

13 *impressive swimmer by the age of six*: Interviews with GG and WG Jr.

14 *pasted into a family album*: Collection of GG.

15 *seven languages*: Interviews with GG and WG Jr.

15 *Rudy's hero, General Józef Piłsudski*: Interview with GG.

15 *Frederik VIII*: Correspondence, collection of GG.

15 *Tootsie*: *New York Daily News* and *New York Daily Sun* (dateless) articles pasted in scrapbook created by FG.

16 Shabbos *goy*: Interview with GG.

17 *budding suffragette*: Ibid.

18 *Babcia*: Interviews with GG and WG Jr.

19 *Bayside, in Queens*: Research on Bayside in the 1920s conducted at the Bayside Historical Society with Alison McKay.

20 *Ford Model A*: Photos, family album.

20 *he befriended the female librarian*: Interview with GG.

23 *Bayside's Hook and Ladder 152 and Engine Company 306*: Private correspondence and "Youth with Byrd Sends Message to Home Friends," *Flushing Journal*, October 13, 1928.

24 *He had a solid B average*: Details of classes from the New York City Board of Education official requirements of interior design students at Textile High, and the Textile High 1928 yearbook, *The Loom*.

25 *Vincent van Gogh and his friend Paul Gauguin*: Interviews with GG and WG Jr., and Billy Gawronski's letters home.

25 *Aurie Aileen Carter . . . Florizel Cunningham*: Gleaned from details and autographs in the Textile High 1928 yearbook, *The Loom*, and interview with GG.

27 *He sought the guidance of Edward Bernays*: Interview with ER.

TWO: GOOD MEN SHOULD APPLY

33 *in a February 1928* Popular Mechanics *article*: J. Olin Howe, "The Bottom of the World," *Popular Mechanics*, February 1928.

33 *forty thousand people had applied to go to Antarctica*: Various sources; best estimate via interview with ER.

34 *But not, Billy noted, a single Pole*: Dan J. Kallen, "Byrd's Polish Stowaway," *Poland*, April 1929.

37 *suite 340*: Byrd stationery, collection of Ohio State University Byrd Polar and Climate Research Center.

38 *first steady girlfriend*: Interview with GG; photographs in her collection.

38 *Billy's senior prom*: Details of Textile High senior prom from the *Textilian*, undated scrapbook clippings, June 1928, and additional coverage in the Textile High 1928 yearbook, *The Loom. The 1928 Loom*, collection of GG.

40 *that commenced Monday, June 18*: *Textilian*, June 1928 scrapbook clippings.

41 *His pet quote*: Interview with GG.

41 *applications from women and girls*: Information about women applicants to the Byrd expedition is from Ohio State University Byrd Polar and Climate Research Center, BAE 1, folder 4393.

44 *Billy had taken his rats to school*: Background on yearbook rat quip from my interviews with GG.

46 *Not many things in the world frightened Amundsen, except his mother*: 2013 lecture, polar historian Carol Knott.

46 *she gave him her special spiritual charm*: Collection of the Józef Piłsudski Institute of America, Brooklyn, NY; interview with GG.

46 *something* vonderful . . . *many amulets*: Interview with WG Jr.

47 *Kurrent*: Postcards from Francesca to her mother from the collection at the Józef Piłsudski Institute of America, Brooklyn, NY. Translation of postcards by Ruth Bloch.

49 *Billy caught sight*: Copy of 1929 speech to Textile High auditorium.

49 *Cooper Union accepted Billy*: Various articles, including O. R. Pilat, "Ship Off for Antarctica as Byrd Explains Liquor Aboard; Stowaway Found," *Brooklyn (NY) Daily Eagle*, August 26, 1928, 1.

50 *His badges included*: Paul A. Siple, *A Boy Scout with Byrd* (New York: G. P. Putnam's Sons, 1931).

52 *meet and greet at Gimbel Brothers*: Interview with GG.

52 *Byrd Hop*: "'Byrd Hop' Divides Dancing Teachers," *New York Times*, August 29, 1928; Ralph Giordano, *Satan in the Dance Hall* (Lanham, MD: Scarecrow Press, 2008).

53 *President Hoover's Belgian shepherd, King Tut*: Clipped scrapbook article, FG.

56 *Diamond brand walnuts*: Ibid.

THREE: THE CITY OF NEW YORK

59 *East River pier at . . . Central Lanes:* Interview with WG Jr.

63 *The whisky was smartly cloned*: Shackleton malt whisky historical details from Mackinlays / Whyte & Mackay corporate office.

66 *Frédéric Auguste Bartholdi*: Elizabeth Mitchell, *Liberty's Torch: The Great Adventure to Build the Statue of Liberty* (New York: Atlantic Monthly Press, 2014).

69 *Jack Solomon was actually Jack Solowitz*: Much of the information on Jack Solowitz comes from interviews with his two adopted sons—Alan Solowitz and Larry Solowitz—as well as from Jewish journals of the day that covered "the Jewish stowaway" widely.

71 *an aerial stowaway on the* Graf Zeppelin: Interviews with Alan and Larry Solowitz; August 26, 1963 *Tampa Times* clipping by Jody Padgett, collection of Alan Solowitz.

73 *The three stowaways quickly*: A very popular article that cemented the story of the multiple stowaways in the public imagination was published in *The Literary Digest*, no author. "A Million-Dollar Attack on the South Pole," September 15, 1928.

FOUR: THE TRIUMPH OF THE CENTURY

76 *"Doomed to Study Interior Decoration"*: O. R. Pilat, *Brooklyn (NY) Daily Eagle*, August 26, 1928, 1.

76 *William Todd's Tebo Yacht Basin*: Charles Cooke and E. B. White, "Tebo Basin," *New Yorker*, April 26, 1930; advertisements in *Motorboarding*, January 1928, 167, 170, 285.

79 Adams's book: Beyond the Barrier with Byrd: An Authentic Story of the Byrd Antarctic Exploring Expedition (Chicago: Goldsmith, 1932).

84 The three-story, high-ceiling, cream-colored Victorian manor: Details on Byrd's childhood home come primarily from the children's biographies listed; also Alden Hatch, The Byrds of Virginia (New York: Holt, Rinehart and Winston, 1969), and vintage postcards.

FIVE: SOUTH POLE OR BUST

91 easy target for pranks: Adams, Beyond the Barrier with Byrd, 81.

103 nicknamed him Captain Klim: Interview with ER.

104 "Oh! I just felt happy": Letters, collection of GG.

108 Settled by Scots in 1848: 1928–30 information on Dunedin comes from brochures and the Dunedin Public Library archives.

SIX: FIRST ICE

117 Asked for his opinion on the pink whale: Adams, Beyond the Barrier, 168.

118 crew members spotted the first emperor penguins: Penguin information comes from my interview with penguin scientist Dr. Gary Miller, conducted in Antarctica, 2013.

121 The good Boy Scout crafted: Interview with ER.

123 long story about Billy: Kallen, "Byrd's Polish Stowaway."

129 A Radiogram that Petersen sent from Billy: Collection of GG.

131 The Matson freighter Golden State: Multiple New Zealand and Australian papers covered Robert White Lanier's arrival and trial, available online at Papers Past, National Library of New Zealand.

135 most treasured possession: Collection of GG.

136 Tennant rustled up meals: Drawn from various speeches, articles, and especially Jason C. Anthony, Hoosh: Roast Penguin, Scurvy Day, and Other Stories of Antarctic Cuisine (Lincoln: University of Nebraska Press, 2012).

137 Bennie Roth became the first to celebrate the Jewish holiday of Passover on the ice: Roth's experiences were wildly covered in the Jewish press from 1928 to 1930, including "Jewish Member of Byrd South

Pole Expedition Had Talith, Tefilim, Sidur with Him," Jewish Telegraphic Agency, June 22, 1930.

SEVEN: THE STOWAWAY REPORT

142 *Bob Lanier, newly acquitted*: Multiple articles online, National Library of New Zealand.

142 *model of Little America*: Interview with GG.

143 *Billy's letter to his folks*: Collection of GG.

EIGHT: FINE ENOUGH

152 *he flew* Miss Silvertown *at record speed*: Multiple Associated Press stories, April 1–7, 1930.

153 *cyclorama of Little America*: "Luna Park Has Huge Cyclorama of Little America, Byrd's Antarctic Base," *New York Times*, May 18, 1930.

156 *("Greeted by Mother: Wife Not on Tug")*: *New York Herald Tribune*, June 20, 1928.

161 *ditty bags and first aid kits*: Research at the Queens Library Seamen's Church Institute Collection, Queens, New York.

167 *Several expedition members, including Billy, were said to want to get into the "flying game"*: Paul Harrison, NEA (Newspaper Enterprise Association) syndicate, "Men of Byrd Expedition Now Are Exploring for New Jobs," July 2, 1930.

168 *Pacific Whaling Company*: Billy in the whale game: *Stella Polaris*. Captain Stenhouse: Emily Dorman.

172 *A reference letter was penned to President Nicholas Murray Butler*: Columbia-related correspondence from Ohio State University Byrd Polar and Climate Research Center, BAE 1, file 6604.

NINE: GREAT DEPRESSION

176 *a free Thanksgiving meal*: Associated Press Wire Service, "Six Old Comrades of Byrd Talk Shop over the Turkey," November 25, 1932.

178 Dar Pomorza: Interview with GG.

178 *Billy gave it one last shot with the admiral*: All correspondence between Byrd and Billy Gawronski comes from Ohio State University Byrd Polar and Climate Research Center, BAE 1, file 6604.

179 *Francesca wrote to Byrd*: Ibid.

184 *The ship had originally headed to Havana*: "Voyage of the St. Louis." United States Holocaust Memorial Museum, https://www.ushmm.org /wlc/en/article.php?ModuleId=10005267.

186 *Today you can still see the upholstered sides of the campus chapel*: Personal tour of US Merchant Marine Academy, Kings Point, NY, with in-house experts.

187 *twenty-three-year-old George Gibbs*: Glenn M. Stein, "George Washington Gibbs Jr.," American National Biography Online, last modified February 2000, www.anb.org/articles/06/06-00895.html.

187 *in the hills of northern Tanganyika*: Interview with GG.

187 *several hundred once-malnourished Polish youngsters*: Information gleaned from photographs, ship logs, Lynne Taylor, *Polish Orphans of Tengeru* (Toronto: Dundurn Press, 2009), and Lucjan Krolikowski, *Stolen Childhood: A Saga of Polish War Children* (San Jose, CA: Authors Choice Press, 1983).

188 *a boy who called himself Tarzan*: Interview with GG.

188 *Billy's favorite poets were the Romantics*: Ibid.

189 *Billy's run was farther north, to ice-free Murmansk*: Information on Billy's time in Murmansk and his general experiences there come from interviews with GG and WG Jr., as well as with George G. Billy, chief librarian, US Merchant Marine Academy, and Captain Kenneth Force, US Merchant Marine Academy, director of music; also Robert Carse, *A Cold Corner of Hell: The Story of the Murmansk Convoys, 1941– 1945* (Garden City, NY: Doubleday, 1969), and Herman E. Rosen, *Gallant Ship, Brave Men: The Heroic Story of a World War II Liberty Ship* (Kings Point, NY: American Merchant Marine Museum, 2003).

191 *a captain's hat made by Wallachs*: Billy's captain's hat from World War II is located in the Józef Piłsudski Institute of America, Brooklyn, NY.

EPILOGUE

194 *Sailing to Taipei, Taiwan . . . In the Italian port of Gioia Tauro*: Interview with GG.

194 *"Dreams of the Sea"*: Ibid.

195 *Billy met the young antiques shop manager Gizela Trawicka*: Ibid.

197 *He and Gizela opened a nursery*: Background on Billy and Gizela's time together in Northport, Long Island, and Cape Elizabeth, Maine, ibid.

SELECTED BIBLIOGRAPHY

BOOKS

Adult Literature

Adams, Harry. *Beyond the Barrier with Byrd: An Authentic Story of the Byrd Antarctic Exploring Expedition.* Chicago: Goldsmith, 1932.

Allen, Frederick Lewis. *Only Yesterday: An Informal History of the 1920s.* New York: Harper & Row., 1931.

Anthony, Jason C. *Hoosh: Roast Penguin, Scurvy Day, and Other Stories of Antarctic Cuisine.* Lincoln: University of Nebraska Press, 2012.

Bertrand, Kenneth J. *Americans in Antarctica, 1775–1948.* New York: American Geographical Society, 1971.

Bown, Stephen R. *The Last Viking: The Life of Roald Amundsen.* Boston: Da Capo Press, 2012.

Bryson, Bill. *One Summer.* New York: Doubleday, 2013.

Bukowczyk, John J. *A History of the Polish Americans.* New Brunswick, NJ: Transaction, 2008.

Bursey, Jack. *Antarctic Night.* London: Longmans, Green, 1957.

Byrd, Richard E. *Skyward.* New York: G. P. Putnam's Sons, 1928.

———. *Little America.* New York: G. P. Putnam's Sons, 1930.

Carse, Robert. *Rum Row: The Liquor Fleet That Fueled the Roaring Twenties.* Mystic, CT: Flat Hammock Press, 1959.

———. *A Cold Corner of Hell: The Story of the Murmansk Convoys, 1941–1945.* Garden City, NY: Doubleday, 1969.

Carter, Paul A. *Little America: Town at the End of the World.* New York: Columbia University Press, 1979.

Cherry-Garrard, Apsley. *The Worst Journey in the World.* London: Constable, 1922.

Church, Ian. *Last Port to Antarctica.* Dunedin, NZ: Otago Heritage Books, 1997.

Foster, Coram. *Rear Admiral Byrd and the Polar Expeditions.* New York: A. L. Burt, 1930.

Giordano, Ralph. *Satan in the Dance Hall.* Lanham, MD: Scarecrow Press, 2008.

Glines, Carroll V. *Bernt Balchen: Polar Aviator.* Washington, DC: Smithsonian Institution Press, 1999.

Gould, Laurence M. *Cold.* New York: Brewer, Warren & Putnam, 1931.

Hatch, Alden. *The Byrds of Virginia.* New York: Holt, Rinehart and Winston, 1969.

Hoyt, Edwin P. *The Last Explorer: The Adventures of Admiral Byrd.* New York: John Day, 1968.

Krolikowski, Lucjan. *Stolen Childhood: A Saga of Polish War Children.* San Jose, CA: Authors Choice Press, 1983.

McKay, Alison. *Bayside.* Mount Pleasant, SC: Arcadia, 2008.

Miller, Francis Trevelyan. *Byrd's Great Adventure.* Chicago: John C. Winston, 1930.

Mortimer, Gavin. *The Great Swim.* New York: Bloomsbury Press, 2008.

Murphy, Charles. *Struggle: The Life of Commander Byrd.* New York: Frederick A. Stokes, 1928.

Owen, Russell. *South of the Sun*. New York: John Day, 1934.

Railey, Hilton H. *Touch'd with Madness*. New York: Carrick & Evans, 1938.

Rodgers, Eugene. *Beyond the Barrier: The Story of Byrd's First Expedition to Antarctica*. Annapolis, MD: Bluejacket Books/Naval Institute Press, 1990.

Rose, Lisle A. *Explorer: The Life of Richard E. Byrd*. Columbia: University of Missouri Press, 2008.

Rosen, Herman E. *Gallant Ship, Brave Men: The Heroic Story of a World War II Liberty Ship*. Kings Point, NY: American Merchant Marine Museum, 2003.

Siple, Paul A. *A Boy Scout with Byrd*. New York: G. P. Putnam's Sons, 1931.

Taylor, Lynne. *Polish Orphans of Tengeru*. Toronto: Dundurn Press, 2009.

Vaughan, Norman D., with Cecil B. Murphey. *With Byrd at the Bottom of the World*. Harrisburg, PA: Stackpole Books, 1992.

Children's Literature

Bursey, Jack. *St. Lunaire: Antarctic Lead Dog*. Grand Rapids, MI: Glory, 1974.

Duble, Kathleen Benner. *The Story of the* Samson. Illustrated by Alexander Farquharson. Watertown, MA: Charlesbridge, 2008.

Green, Fitzhugh. *Dick Byrd: Air Explorer*. New York: G. P. Putnam's Sons, 1928.

Macdonald, W. A. *A Farewell to Commander Byrd*. New York: Coward-McCann, 1929.

O'Brien, John S. *By Dogsled for Byrd*. Chicago: Follett, 1931.

Rink, Paul. *Conquering Antarctica: Admiral Richard E. Byrd*. Chicago: Encyclopædia Britannica Press, 1961.

Ross, M. I., ed., *South of Zero: The Journal of John Hale Meredith While with the Clark-Jamison Antarctic Expedition*. New York: Literary Guild, 1932.

Seiple, Samantha. *Byrd & Igloo*. New York: Scholastic Press, 2013.

Smith, Dean C. *By the Seat of My Pants*. Boston: Atlantic Monthly Press, 1961.

Steinberg, Alfred. *Admiral Richard E. Byrd*. New York: Van Rees Press, 1960.

Strong, Charles E. *We Were There with Byrd at the South Pole*. New York: Grosset & Dunlap, 1956.

Van Riper, Guernsey. *Richard Byrd: Boy of the South Pole*. Indianapolis: Bobbs-Merrill, 1958.

———. *Richard Byrd: Boy Who Braved the Unknown*. Illustrated by Aubrey Combs. Indianapolis: Bobbs-Merrill, 1958.

West, Wallace. *With Admiral Byrd in Little America*. Racine, WI: Whitman, 1934.

Wilson, Patricia Potter, and Roger Leslie. *Eagle on Ice*. New York: Vantage Press, 2008.

BOOKLETS

Owen, Russell. *The Barque "City of New York."* New York: *New York Times*, 1930.

SELECTED ARTICLES

Note: The *New York Times* was the official newspaper of the first Byrd expedition, and covered the related events almost daily. I consulted numerous *Times* articles, mainly by Russell Owen, who won the Pulitzer Prize for his reporting. Joe de Ganahl, who traveled on the *Eleanor Bolling* and served as auxiliary reporter, authored several key stories that mentioned or featured Billy Gawronski.

In addition, the following of many articles consulted stood out:

Brooklyn (NY) Daily Eagle. "The Happiest Boy: Persistent Stowaway Succeeds in Joining Byrd Expedition." September 25, 1928.

———. "Bayside Stowaway Fights Ice with Byrd, Writes He Is Happy." December 27, 1928.

Byrd, Commander Richard E. "Why I Am Going to the South Pole." *World's Work*, December 1927.

Cleveland Plain Dealer. "Romance of Greasy Pots." September 29, 1928.

Columbia University Alumni News. "Two College Students with Byrd in the Antarctic." November 14, 1930.

Columbia (University) Spectator. "Freshmen Represent 21 States, 5 Nations." November 10, 1930.

Flushing (NY) Journal. "Bayside Boy Is Forcibly Removed from Byrd's Ship." September 21, 1928.

———. "South Pole or Bust: Bayside Boy with Byrd Telegraphs Father Here." October 6, 1928.

———. "Youth with Byrd Sends Message to Home Friends." October 13, 1928.

———. "Parents Receive Word from Son." November 2, 1928.

Green, Fitzhugh. "The Mother of Tom, Dick, and Harry." *American*, February 1928.

———. "Dick Byrd, Adventurer." *Popular Science*, May–September 1928.

Harlow, Winifred Webster. "*Aviation Breeding Eagle-Eyed Race!*" *New York Evening Graphic*, March 31, 1928.

Harrison, Paul. "Men of Byrd Expedition Now Are Exploring for New Jobs." NEA (Newspaper Enterprise Association) syndicate, July 2, 1930.

Healey, Floyd J. "Part of Byrd Expedition Back." *Los Angeles Times*, April 13, 1929.

Howe, J. Olin. "The Bottom of the World." *Popular Mechanics*, February 1928.

Kallen, Dan J. "Byrd's Polish Stowaway." *Poland*, April 1929.

Meinholtz, Fred. "Hello Little America: New York Calling." *Radio News*, July 1929.

New York Daily News. "Goes Up in the World: Tootsie, Now Owned by William Gavronski—Won a Prize in Show of Stray Dogs and Cats." April 21, 1925.

New York Daily News. "Stowaway Wins His Goal, Along to Pole with Byrd." September 26, 1928.

New York Morning-World. "Regular Antarctic Job Given to Boy Stowaway." September 25, 1928.

New York Sun. "Prize Winners Developed from Stray Dogs: William Gavronski with Tootsie." April 21, 1925.

New York World. "Lad's Persistence Rewarded by Byrd." October 6, 1928.

O'Hara, Neal. "With Byrd in the Antarctic by J. Herman Seidlitz," Telling the World (syndicated column), 1928–1929.

Pilat, O. R. "Ship Off for Antarctica as Byrd Explains Liquor Aboard; Stowaway Found." *Brooklyn (NY) Daily Eagle*, August 26, 1928.

———. "Byrd Return Ends Anxiety of Men's Kin." *Brooklyn (NY) Daily Eagle*, March 16, 1930.

———. "Brooklyn Extends Tumultuous Welcome to Byrd and South Polar Crew." *Brooklyn (NY) Daily Eagle*, June 27, 1930.

Pittsburgh Post-Gazette. "Success of a Stowaway." September 27, 1928.

Portland (ME) Press Herald. "Obituary, Capt. William G. Gawronski." May 20, 1981.

Queens (NY) Daily Star. "Bayside Youth Wins Argument: Will Go to Pole." September 26, 1928.

———. "Bayside Youth Tells of Hardship and Heroism Within Antarctic Circle." April 24, 1929.

Richmond (VA) News Leader. "N.Y. Throngs Roar Welcome to Byrd." June 19, 1930.

San Diego Union. "Persistent Stowaway to Go to Antarctic with Com. Byrd." September 26, 1928.

Scientific American. "Stocking Up on Expedition's Larders." November 1928.

St. Louis Post-Dispatch. "Stowaway with Byrd Expedition Feted." April 25, 1929.

Universal Syndicate. "Youth Finally Wins Place with Byrd's Expedition." September 26, 1928.

Virginian-Pilot (Norfolk, VA). "Long Island Youth Insists on Making Trip to Antarctica." September 21, 1928.

———. "Twice Stowaway, Twice Set Ashore, Bill Gawronski Now Full-Fledged Member of Byrd Polar Expedition." September 25, 1928.

Wroblewski, Larry. "Polish Falcons: A Historical Stretch." *Polish American Journal*, July 1985.

PERSONALLY CONDUCTED ORAL INTERVIEWS

Ann Beyer, Gizela Gawronski (many), William Gawronski Jr. (many), Earl Mealins, Eugene Rodgers, Alan Solowitz, Larry Solowitz.

MISCELLANEOUS SOURCES

Copies of William Gawronski speeches, including his 1929 WOR radio address; 1929 and 1930 Textile High School addresses; and various others, 1929, 1930.

Early notebooks of William Gawronski.

Letter from William Gawronski to a Mr. Mystlowski in Poland, who had inquired about his history on the expedition; his file copy, March 12, 1978.

Letters from William Gawronski (private collection of Gizela Gawronski).

Log books of Captain William Gawronski.

Multiple Radiograms from Little America, 1928 to 1930 (private collection of Gizela Gawronski).

Resumes of William Gawronski.

Scrapbook of Francesca Gawronski, 1925 to 1930.

Textile High School yearbook, *The Loom*, 1928.

Various issues of the Textile High newspaper, the *Textilian*, especially the report on the June 15, 1928, prom.

SITES OF RESEARCH

American Victory Ship Mariners Memorial Museum, Tampa; Bayside Historical Society, Bayside, NY; Cape Elizabeth Historical Preservation Society, Cape Elizabeth, ME; Columbia University Libraries, New York; Dartmouth College Library Archives, Hanover, NH; Dunedin Library, Dunedin, New Zealand; Explorers Club, New York; Floyd Bennett Field, Brooklyn, NY; Józef Piłsudski Institute of America, Brooklyn, NY; Library of Congress, Washington, DC; Long Island Historical Society, Brooklyn, NY; Madison Correctional Institution, Madison, FL;

National Archives, Washington, DC; New York Public Library Manuscript and Archives Division, New York; Northport Historical Society, Northport, NY; Ohio State University Byrd Polar and Climate Research Center, Columbus, OH; Polk County Florida South Jail, Frostproof, FL; Port Chalmers Library, Dunedin, New Zealand; Queens Library Seamen's Church Institute Collection, Queens, NY; St. Josephat Church, Bayside, NY; St. Stanislaus Church, New York; US Merchant Marine Academy, Kings Point, NY.

PHOTO CREDITS

15. *The New York Times* and *St. Louis Post-Dispatch*
16. Ohio State University Archives/Byrd Polar and Climate Research Center
17. Ohio State University Archives/Byrd Polar and Climate Research Center
18. Ohio State University Archives/Byrd Polar and Climate Research Center
19. *The New York Times* and *St. Louis Post-Dispatch*
20. *The New York Times* and *St. Louis Post-Dispatch*
21. National Archives and Records Administration
22. *The New York Times* and *St. Louis Post-Dispatch*
23. Ohio State University Archives/Byrd Polar and Climate Research Center
24. *The New York Times* and *St. Louis Post-Dispatch*
25. *The New York Times* and *St. Louis Post-Dispatch*
26. Ohio State University Archives/Byrd Polar and Climate Research Center
27. *The New York Times*
28. Ohio State University Archives/Byrd Polar and Climate Research Center
29. Associated Press
30. From the New York Public Library
31. Sony/ATV
32. Gizela Gawronski & Józef Piłsudski Institute of America
33. Gizela Gawronski & Józef Piłsudski Institute of America
34. Gizela Gawronski
35. Gizela Gawronski & Józef Piłsudski Institute of America
36. Gizela Gawronski & Józef Piłsudski Institute of America
37. Gizela Gawronski & Józef Piłsudski Institute of America
38. Gizela Gawronski & Józef Piłsudski Institute of America

INDEX

ABOUT THE AUTHOR

LAURIE GWEN SHAPIRO is a native of New York City's Lower East Side, where she still lives with her Aussie husband, fifteen-year-old daughter, and elderly father, who used to swim in the East River. She has most recently written articles for publications including *New York*, *Slate*, *Aeon*, and the *Los Angeles Review of Books*, and has her own history column focusing on unsung heroes for *The Forward*. Shapiro is also a documentary filmmaker who won an Independent Spirit Award for directing IFC's *Keep the River on Your Right: A Modern Cannibal Tale* and an Emmy nomination for producing HBO's *Finishing Heaven*. This is her first nonfiction book.